For the individual who suffers ur
Deepak Reju serves you well by p
in the gospel of Jesus Christ. He
the month, enabling you to grow
self, your circumstances, and God. Through daily reading and
reflection questions, Deepak provides you with the necessary
insight and practical application to break pornography's hold,
helping you to better glorify God in your daily living.

    —**Kevin Carson**, Pastor, Sonrise Baptist Church, Ozark, Mis-
souri; Biblical Counseling Professor and Department Chair,
Baptist Bible College and Theological Seminary, Springfield,
Missouri

There are a number of books that tell you what to do if you want
to kick your porn habit. *Pornography: Fighting for Purity* is different. It doesn't leave you to get on with it yourself; instead, it walks
with you through the process. Day by day, over thirty-one days,
it will lead you away from porn and back to Christ. This is not a
self-help book that demands more effort before inevitably leading
to more failure. The book is filled with gospel grace and therefore
with gospel hope. I warmly encourage you to read it. Better still,
read it with a mature Christian.

    —**Tim Chester**, Pastor, Grace Church, Boroughbridge, UK;
author, *Closing the Window: Steps to Living Porn Free*

Here is medicine in the form of meditations; a weapon in the
shape of a thirty-one-day devotional. Begin each day, for a month,
with Deepak reading you and teaching you from Scripture. Plain-
spoken, searching, practical, humble, and hopeful—this could be
just what you've been looking for in your struggle for something
better than fantasy.

    —**Mark Dever**, Senior Pastor, Capitol Hill Baptist Church,
Washington, D.C.; President, 9Marks

Anyone knows that, in order to conquer any sin, we must attack that problem at its core—intentionally and deliberately. An old Valley of Vision prayer says that "if we would have any sin subdued, we must not only labor to overcome it . . . but must invite Christ to abide in its place." In *Pornography: Fighting for Purity*, Deepak Reju has helped men, in a very practical way, to do this very thing!

—**John Freeman**, Founder, Harvest USA; Author, *Hide or Seek: When Men Get Real with God About Sex*

Deepak Reju frankly and pastorally addresses one of the most pervasive, most lethal, and least acknowledged assaults on Christian discipleship today. Since shame and self-condemnation cannot free those who are enslaved to lust in its various easily accessible forms, Reju's month of meditations fortifies those who are committed to fight for purity by focusing our hearts' eyes on Christ in all his beauty, mercy, and power.

—**Dennis E. Johnson**, Professor of Practical Theology, Westminster Seminary California

PORNOGRAPHY

31-DAY DEVOTIONALS FOR LIFE

A Series

DEEPAK REJU
Series Editor

Addictive Habits: Changing for Good, by David R. Dunham
After an Affair: Pursuing Restoration, by Michael Scott Gembola
Anger: Calming Your Heart, by Robert D. Jones
Anxiety: Knowing God's Peace, by Paul Tautges
Assurance: Resting in God's Salvation, by William P. Smith
Chronic Illness: Walking by Faith, by Esther Smith
Contentment: Seeing God's Goodness, by Megan Hill
Doubt: Trusting God's Promises, by Elyse Fitzpatrick
Engagement: Preparing for Marriage, by Mike McKinley
Fearing Others: Putting God First, by Zach Schlegel
Grief: Walking with Jesus, by Bob Kellemen
Marriage Conflict: Talking as Teammates, by Steve Hoppe
Money: Seeking God's Wisdom, by Jim Newheiser
Pornography: Fighting for Purity, by Deepak Reju

PORNOGRAPHY

FIGHTING
FOR
PURITY

DEEPAK REJU

PUBLISHING
P.O. BOX 817 • PHILLIPSBURG • NEW JERSEY 08865-0817

Library of Congress Cataloging-in-Publication Data

Names: Reju, Deepak, 1969- author.
Title: Pornography : fighting for purity / Deepak Reju.
Description: Phillipsburg, New Jersey : P&R Publishing Company, [2018] |
  Series: 31-day devotionals for life | Includes bibliographical references.
Identifiers: LCCN 2018027283| ISBN 9781629953632 (pbk.) | ISBN 9781629953649
  (epub) | ISBN 9781629953656 (mobi)
Subjects: LCSH: Pornography--Religious aspects--Christianity--Prayers and
  devotions. | Sex addiction--Religious aspects--Christianity--Prayers and devotions.
Classification: LCC BV4597.6 .R45 2018 | DDC 241/.667--dc23
LC record available at https://lccn.loc.gov/2018027283

Contents

Tips for Reading This Devotional

EARLY IN OUR MARRIAGE, my wife and I lived on the top floor of a town house, in a small one-bedroom apartment. Whenever it rained, leaks in the roof would drip through the ceiling and onto our floors. I remember placing buckets in different parts of the apartment and watching the water slowly drip, one drop at a time. I put large buckets out and thought, *It'll take a while to fill them.* The water built up over time, and often I was surprised at how quickly those buckets filled up, overflowing if I didn't pay close enough attention.

This devotional is just like rain filling up a bucket. It's slow, and it builds over time. Just a few verses every day. Drip. Drip. Drip. Just a few drops of Scripture daily to satiate your parched soul.

We start with Scripture. God's Word is powerful. In fact, it's the most powerful force in the entire universe.[1] It turns the hearts of kings, brings comfort to the lowly, and gives spiritual sight to the blind. It transforms lives and turns them upside down. We know that the Bible is God's very own words, so we read and study it to know God himself.

Our study of Scripture is practical. Theology should change how we live. It's crucial to connect the Word with your struggles. Often, as you read this devotional, you'll see the word *you* because I speak directly to you, the reader. Each reading contains reflection questions and a practical suggestion. You'll get much more from this experience if you answer the questions and do the practical exercises. Don't skip them. Do them for the sake of your own soul.

Our study of Scripture is worshipful. Fundamentally, any struggle with pornography and masturbation is a worship problem.

We've lost our orientation toward the One who should rule our lives, and we need to turn back to him. The Word points us to Christ, who rescues us from our plight and reorients our life. The goal of your time in God's Word should always be worship. As you grow in your affections for Christ, the King, you put to death your affections for pornography and masturbation. The power of a greater affection for Christ can transform your soul. Adore Christ. Love him. Cherish him. Praise him. Honor him. Give your whole life to him. Don't hold anything back.

If you find this devotional helpful (and I trust that you will!), reread it in different seasons of your life. Work through it this coming month, and then come back to it a year from now, to remind yourself how to do battle with sexual sin.

This devotional is *not* meant to be a comprehensive guide to fighting pornography and masturbation. Good volumes are already written for that purpose. Buy them and make good use of them. You'll see several resources listed at the end of the book.

That's enough for now. Let's begin.

Deepak Reju

Introduction

Your Need

A man named Jairus, who was the ruler of a synagogue, came to Jesus and fell at his feet. He was desperate, for his only daughter was sick and dying. He wanted Jesus to come because he knew that, if Jesus laid his hands on her, "she will live" (Matt. 9:18).

Not long after that, a sick woman came to Jesus. She had been bleeding for twelve years, and she had spent her living on physicians. Twelve years of medical assistance amounted to nothing (Luke 8:43). Immersed in a crowd, she pressed through to see Jesus and touch his garment. He had the power to change everything.

Some days later, a father came to Jesus, begging him to look at his only child. The boy was possessed by an evil spirit, convulsing and foaming at the mouth (Luke 9:38–39). The father had gone to Jesus's disciples, but they had failed to expel the spirit. He was coming to Jesus as his only hope.

Read the gospels, and you will see that they keep coming. Needy people—distressed, despairing, beyond hope, and looking to Jesus. They are looking for a Rescuer, Healer, and Redeemer.

You are not unlike them. If you opened this book, it's because you need Jesus just like they did. You are struggling with pornography and masturbation, and you need help. If this is true, then welcome. Jesus is waiting for you.

Your Problem

Ed Welch speaks of *voluntary slavery* to describe your plight.[1] This helpfully captures your problem in two words: you've *voluntarily* chosen sexual sin so often that it now *enslaves* you. A wise friend told me, "What you open yourself up to will eventually control your heart."

Lust is desire that is disordered and out of control.[2] Your heart is probably attached to the wrong things, so a vital part of your battle against lust will be to reorient your affections to the right things—not self-fulfillment, but glorifying God; not sex, but purity; not images on a screen, but real people; not guilty pleasures, but joy in heaven.

The chief means of fighting your disordered desires is a growing affection for Christ. Fight fire with fire—fight the sin of lust with a greater love for Christ.[3]

But there is more to the problem. Guilt, shame, self-condemnation, lies, self-justification, confusion, emotional distance from God and others, little time in the Word, doubt, pride—all these factors combine with your disordered affections to put you in a terrible place. It's a hot, complicated mess.

The Bible clearly condemns sexual sin (1 Cor. 5:9–10; 6:9–10; Gal. 5:19; Eph. 5:3, 5; Col. 3:5). You know it's wrong, but you feel trapped, and you need a pathway out. What are you to do about it?

Your Anchor

The natural human tendency is to seek a way out by depending on yourself. *I made this mess, so I'll fix it.* You read books, go to church, implement monitoring software, and find accountability. While these are all fine things to do, they are not enough if you profess Christ. Fix-it strategies put the full weight and responsibility on your shoulders, and as you will find out, that's not a sustainable plan. It might help you temporarily, but it won't get you to the finish line.

This is where Christ enters in. He offers you an invitation.

Come to me, all you who are weary and burdened, and I will give you rest. Take my yoke upon you and learn from me, for I

10

am gentle and humble in heart, and you will find rest for your souls. For my yoke is easy and my burden is light. (Matt. 11:28–30 NIV)

You are tired and weary from the ongoing battle with pornography and masturbation, so Jesus offers you rest. He can be an anchor in this storm, if you repent of your sins and turn to him in faith.

The seed from which all Christianity springs is this good news: *Christ died for sinners.* To survive this battle against pornography, you've got to build your whole life on this truth. Either Christ is worth everything or he is worth nothing at all. There is no middle ground. Lukewarm faith is not faith. Jesus gave his life, conquering sin and death, so that you might have life in him. Will you give your entire life—everything you have—to him?

If you are not a follower of Christ, or if you are not sure whether you are, know that giving your life to Christ is the most important thing you could ever do. Trusting in Jesus is not a religious crutch. It's a personal relationship with the Son of God who came to earth to rescue you from your rebellion against God. "For God so loved the world, that he gave his only Son, that whoever believes in him should not perish but have eternal life" (John 3:16). The conversation about fighting pornography begins and ends with Christ.

Your Goal

The goal of the Christian life is to run the race and make it to the finish line. With God's help, a true believer will persevere to the end.

In his letter to the church in Philippi, Paul writes, "Forgetting what lies behind and straining forward to what lies ahead, I press on toward the goal for the prize of the upward call of God in Christ Jesus" (Phil. 3:13–14). As a runner runs, he's no longer concerned with where he came from.[4] Every muscle in his body is straining forward to what lies ahead. His eyes are focused on a goal: the finish line. He sprints to the end in order to earn the prize (1 Cor. 9:24). This runner's prize is God's calling him heavenward. So also you need to be like this runner—not dwelling on the past, but future-minded. Forget what's behind you; keep your eyes set on heaven.

What's your goal in life? Does it at all resemble the apostle Paul's future-oriented living? Or are you feeling stuck in your sin? Enduring through the difficulties of this life includes fighting sexual sin and living a life of purity. But that's not a one-day battle or a battle for one season. You'll need to fight this battle for the rest of your life.

Having living examples helps. I know godly, mature men who faithfully serve their churches, but who years ago struggled deeply with pornography. Do you know what I notice about them? Consistently, what I see in these men is *a growing affection for and commitment to Christ.* Sustained gospel contact, day in and day out, is the normal rhythm of their lives. The gospel is the air they breathe as they pore over the Word and beg God for mercy. It's their union with Christ, not their own efforts, that keeps them living by faith.

Faith in Christ doesn't leave these men passive or irresponsible; it leads them to greater obedience. Consistently, what I see in these men is *vigilance for the rest of their lives.* A white-knuckling approach—in which you fight sin solely by your own strength—won't get you very far. These men's vigilance is the fruit of a genuine faith. Years removed from the problem, these godly men still maintain transparency with close friends, have accountability software on all their electronic devices, and continue to fight for holy living. Does that surprise you? It shouldn't. In fact, it's a mark of their maturity. They understand the importance of never letting down their guard, because they know how sin can ruin their lives. They are well prepared—with the Word, the Spirit dwelling in them, a good church community, a sober perspective about their sin, and great joy in Christ—to run the race to the very end.

What about you? What would it take for you to follow in their example?

DAY 1

The War for Your Soul

*Beloved, I urge you as sojourners and exiles
to abstain from the passions of the flesh, which wage
war against your soul. (1 Peter 2:11)*

IF YOU'VE PICKED up this book, it's probably because you are
in the middle of a war. It's the *devil's* war—and his weapons are
anger, hatred, lying, selfishness, deceit, confusion, unbelief, and
idolatry. And, in your case, pornography. Over the course of time,
you look at the forbidden—click, click, click. And you feel drawn
back, as if a magnetic pull were dragging you in. You hate it but
want more. You feel ashamed and struggle to find God's forgiveness. Your desires run amok. You get further enslaved. It becomes
the preeminent battle for you.

The battleground of a Christian war is your heart. There are
no terrorists chopping off heads and claiming another country's
sovereign territory. There is no double agent undermining your
homeland. *This is a war for your soul.* And, like most wars, it is
fought to be won or lost. There is no peacekeeping treaty. God is
jealous for your heart, and he is not going to concede this territory to the devil (Jer. 31:33).

Peter asked the Christians of his day to refrain from the selfish passions of their sinful nature. Surrounded by the *ungodly*
practices and customs of unbelievers, the Christians were to live
as sojourners or exiles. They didn't belong, and so their lifestyle
was supposed to look different. The same goes for you—this
world is not your home, and the practices of this world, such as
the destructive habits of pornography and masturbation, should
be foreign to you as a Christian. But, alas, *they are not.*

What is the purpose of a war? To destroy the enemy. The

selfish passions of your flesh are waging war—literally *to destroy* your soul. Scary, isn't it? The war raging inside you is between the Holy Spirit and your sinful flesh. You stare at a computer screen, with a tantalizing image staring back at you, and your flesh rages: "I want more." "Yes, this feels good." "Just a little bit longer." "Forget the truth, for a moment, and enjoy this." "God will forgive me." Click, click, click—you take in more. But with each click, with each stare, with each selfish desire that is fed, the flesh wars against your soul and you sear your conscience with your sin.

Depressing, isn't it? But there is hope. The fact that you picked up this book shows that the battle is not lost. You're still in the fight, and God stands alongside you, claiming to be the victor of your soul. Remember, the Scriptures say, "[God] yearns jealously over the spirit that he has made to dwell in us" (James 4:5). God is jealous for you. He put his Spirit in you, and he is eager to see your spirit worship him for all eternity.

Welcome to the war for your soul. This is your call to arms, and a reminder that God stands alongside you, arm-to-arm, in the fight (2 Tim. 4:16–18). Sound the trumpet, and let's begin.

Reflect: Have you given up? If so, does it give you any hope that God "yearns jealously" for you? Remember: you are not alone. God has not given up on you.

Reflect: Because Christ died for you, you don't have to give up.

Act: Write a few sentences about what it would mean for you to be an exile or sojourner in this world.

DAY 2

What Is Your True Identity?

*For you did not receive the spirit of slavery to fall back into fear,
but you have received the Spirit of adoption as sons, by whom
we cry, "Abba! Father!" The Spirit himself bears witness with
our spirit that we are children of God. (Rom. 8:15–16)*

WHO ARE YOU? Are you a husband or wife, a son or daughter?
Are you a friend? Are you an employee or a student? Are you a
church member? Are you a parent, a brother or sister, or a neighbor? Are you a city or country dweller? Are you a sinner, saint,
or sufferer? What words most describe you? What labels fit you
best? Take a moment and write a few descriptors for yourself in
the margin.

I often look into the face of someone struggling with pornography and ask, "How much does this sin define you?" *Do you
see yourself fundamentally as a porn struggler or as a child of God?*
Which one defines you? When you wake up, what do you think
about first: the images that you viewed last night, or Christ's love
for you? When you walk to work, what defines you: your sense of
shame, or your sense of being an adopted child of God?

Your battle with porn puts it at the forefront of your heart and
mind, so you over-identify with the sin. The selfish desires of your
flesh define you *too much*. Confusion, doubts, shame, or self-hate
push your Christian identity into the background.

Many years ago, a wise friend said to me, "Be who you are." If
you trust in Christ, you are a child of God—whether you sense
that or not. Live as if it is true, because it is.

*Who you are in Christ is your truest, deepest, and most fundamen-
tal identity.* Slow down and reflect on that sentence. Do you really
believe it's true? What is stopping you from believing it fully? If

you trust in Christ and are fighting to repent, you are a child of God. Remember that Spirit-driven sense of being a Christian, and begin to live like it is true . . . because *it is true.* Live as if you are forgiven and cleansed by Christ's blood, because that is who you are.

The apostle Paul told the Christians at Rome that those who yield to the Spirit are sons and daughters of God. If you learn to walk according to the Spirit, you will no longer be a slave to your sins. Does that sound impossible? You don't have to be a slave to pornography. Do you *really* believe that? Can that *really* be true? God's Spirit in you bears witness with your spirit that you really are a child of God. They work together to cry out, "Abba! Father!"

So who are you? If you wrote, "I'm a child of God," you're off to a good start. If you didn't, don't be scared. Even now, you can yield to the Spirit (Rom. 8:14), ground yourself in God's Word (Ps. 1:2), and cling to God's people (Prov. 18:24). They will help you to "be who you are": a child of God.

Reflect: How much does your sexual sin define you? Does it over-define you? If so, ask God for mercy (Ps. 130:2) and confess your sin to him (Prov. 28:13–14).

Reflect: Ask God to grant you hope *in Christ.*

Act: Find a committed, mature Christian and ask this person about his or her identity. When the answer comes, "I'm a Christian," press further and ask, "How do you know?" Then ask for help with how you can grow in your own Spirit-driven sense of being a child of God. Look at Scripture together and pray together about your identity in Christ.

DAY 3

Walking by the Spirit

If we live by the Spirit, let us also walk by the Spirit. (Gal. 5:25)

WHO IS IN charge of your life? Are you following the desires of your flesh and the pressures of this world? Or are you being led by the Spirit?

Living by faith through the Spirit and putting your sin to death are two sides of the same coin. But one drives the other. As you live according to the Spirit's strength and direction, God gives you the power to put to death the sinful desires of your flesh.

When you were born again, the Holy Spirit took up residence in you. He gives you life. So we "live by the Spirit" (Gal. 5:25).

Since we live by the Spirit, we need to follow his lead. Walking by the Spirit, as the verse goes on to instruct us, pictures walking in a row or marching in a line. Think about a soldier marching in step as his sergeant barks out orders. The cadence of the sergeant's orders bellow out ("Step . . . step . . . step . . . step . . . step . . . step"), and the soldier's every step is in accordance with his directions. The soldier stays in the formation, and all he needs to do is obey the sergeant's instructions. The NIV appropriately translates this as "Let us keep *in step* with the Spirit."[1] The Spirit leads, and all you need to do is follow his lead.

But you don't do this by yourself. The apostle Paul is not barking out orders to you while watching from a safe, smug distance. He is marching in the same formation. Paul says, "Let *us* walk by the Spirit." He includes himself. You're not alone. In fact, in this line is a host of other believers fighting the same battle and marching in step with you.

We can walk in obedience if we let the Spirit lead. Do you believe that that's true? Or have you given in to your sinful nature so often that you've given up hope? Consistent victory over the flesh is possible, but it comes only from the Spirit's lead. "Walk by the Spirit, and you will not gratify the desires of the flesh" (Gal. 5:16).

Who is setting the agenda for your life—your sinful flesh, or the Spirit? Be honest. When you wake up in the morning, how self-reliant are you? Do you walk into the day with your game plan, your desires, your dreams, your goals, your expectations, and your schemes charting the course? Or do you turn to God and say, "Lord God, I need your help"; "Holy Spirit, come and lead the way"; "I can't do this on my own—only you can"? When's the last time these phrases came out of your mouth? Do you pray these kinds of prayers in humility, pleading for the Spirit to direct your life?

Don't wait any longer. Give up your own schemes and follow the Spirit's lead in your life. You can't defeat this problem through your own power; it can only be done through the Holy Spirit's strength.

Reflect: What goals, dreams, hopes, and agendas do you need to give up right now in order to let the Spirit take control of your life?

Act: Don't let another moment pass without turning to God and asking for the Spirit's help. Pray now, with humility, begging God to set the agenda for your life. Commit to following the Spirit's lead. Write out a prayer below asking for God's help.

DAY 4

Digging into Your Heart

"No good tree bears bad fruit, nor does a bad tree bear good fruit. . . .
A good man brings good things out of the good stored up in his heart,
and an evil man brings evil things out of the evil stored up in his heart.
For the mouth speaks what the heart is full of." (Luke 6:43, 45 NIV)

WHAT MOTIVATES YOU? What makes you tick? In Luke 6, Jesus turns into a botanist and gives an extended excursus about trees and fruit. His point is not to tell us about plants and vegetation but to teach us why we do what we do. What goals and desires define what you do each day?

Jesus teaches us three things. First, *each tree is known by its fruit.* How do you recognize the types of trees that are planted in your yard? By their fruit! You look at a tree with luscious apples hanging from it and say, "That's an apple tree!" Good trees don't bear bad fruit, and bad trees don't bear good fruit. Figs don't come from thorn bushes, and grapes are not picked from briers (Luke 6:44). This is the rule of recognition. You know a tree by the fruit it produces. So also with your life—we can tell a lot about you by the fruit you produce.

What is the term *fruit* referring to? In this text, *fruit* refers to what you say. But fruit is everything that flows from your heart—your words, your thoughts, your actions, your feelings, your plans and dreams.

Second, *the tree determines the fruit.* Good trees produce good fruit; bad trees produce bad fruit. There is a relationship between the *nature* of the tree and the *quality* of fruit it produces. So also your character determines the kind of life that you live.

Third, *your heart determines your life.* Jesus says that your life flows out of your heart. If you've stored up good in your heart, good flows out. If you've stored up evil, evil flows out. Have you ever said something and then thought, "I didn't mean that" or "That came out of nowhere"? What you said didn't come out of "nowhere"; it came from your heart!

Why does this matter? Often, as you struggle with pornography, you are tempted to address the fruit of your life, not your heart. You can get so caught up with rearranging the circumstances of your life—such as installing internet filter programs, adjusting your daily schedule, guarding your eyes, and thinking carefully about your living situation. While these things are important, they don't define *why* you do what you do. To figure out what motivates you, we need to dig into your heart.

What is going on in your heart? Is there a greedy and reckless pursuit of pleasure? Does porn fill the boredom of your pious lifestyle? Are you looking for adventure? Are you angry at God for not giving you a boyfriend or girlfriend? Are you frustrated with God for not giving you a way to satisfy your sexual needs? Are you looking for affirmation or comfort? Are you looking to escape the stress, pain, or disappointment of your life? If none of these things fit, what does motivate you?

Reflect: What do your words, thoughts, and actions reveal about your heart? Is it healthy or sick?

Reflect: What brings you joy? What gets you up in the morning? Where do you find hope? How you answer these questions tells you a lot about your heart.

Act: Find a wise, mature Christian friend or pastor, and ask him or her to help you draw out the deep purposes of your heart (Prov. 20:5).

DAY 5

Be Radical

"You have heard that it was said, 'You shall not commit adultery.'
But I say to you that everyone who looks at a woman with lustful
intent has already committed adultery with her in his heart.
If your right eye causes you to sin, tear it out and throw it away.
For it is better that you lose one of your members than that
your whole body be thrown into hell." (Matt. 5:27–29)

JESUS REMINDS YOU about the seventh commandment:
do not commit adultery. But he takes it one step further. What
leads you to commit adultery is the lustful intent in your heart.
In Scripture, the term *heart* is used to describe the core of who
you are (Prov. 4:23; 27:19; Luke 6:45). Lust, coveting, and greed
are heart problems. You don't need to touch a woman to commit
sin. You merely need to look at her lustfully. This says something
about your heart, doesn't it? You've got a *sick* heart.

Jesus goes on: If your eye causes you to sin, tear it out. Obvi-
ously our Lord uses exaggeration for effect. The point is not to
actually harm yourself but to understand how serious sexual sin
is. Christ uses graphic imagery to say, *be radical when you deal with*
your sexual sin.

Pause and think. How radical are you as you fight sin? Consider the options. Maybe you don't do anything about it, because
you don't want to give up the sin. Maybe you've felt a tinge of guilt,
and even more shame, but you keep coming back for more. Maybe
you've told a friend about the images or videos you have looked
at, but you haven't gotten rid of your access. So long as you allow
yourself access to pornography—so long as you don't prevent this
black bile from seeping into your heart—you're doing great harm
to your life.

Christ said to *be radical*. Measure your last few months against Jesus's words. Have you taken drastic measures to fight the sin, or have you made excuses, delayed making adjustments, or continued to hide the sin rather than confess it? Have you tolerated the sin, coddled it, maybe even welcomed it—and, in so doing, continued to give it a chance to hurt your life?

What is better: to lose an eye but walk toward heaven, or to run toward hell? Christ warns you. His mention of hell should scare you. If you choose to indulge the sin, to ignore God's commands, to disobey and shake your fist at God, then your *rebellion* and *foolishness* will lead to death.[1]

Fighting sin is serious business. Remember, you are at war. Don't tolerate the sin anymore. Cut off any access points to pornography *today*.

Reflect: What is your approach to sin? Measure your life against Jesus's words. Have you taken drastic steps? Are you serious about fighting sin? How can you tell? Or have you been lazy, passive, greedy, or tolerant of the sin? What excuses have you made?

Reflect: What access points have you left open that you haven't closed yet? What *radical* steps can you take *today*?

Act: It's often your solo attempts to fight sin that lead to repeated falls back into temptation. Get help. Tell a friend specific steps you can take to cut off your sin, and ask him or her to check on you to make sure you have done what is needed.

DAY 6

Greater Joy

You make known to me the path of life; in your presence there is fullness of joy; at your right hand are pleasures forevermore. (Ps. 16:11)

HERE ARE A few things I can find delight in:

- I love it when I get home and my three-year-old son rushes to the door, wraps his arms around my legs, and screams, "Daddy's home!"
- I revel in good food—a pizza with fresh crust, salty cheese, and all-natural ingredients or a sizzling, home-cooked, tender steak.
- I enjoy an hour getting sucked into a well-written novel.
- I marvel at the size and breadth of the Grand Canyon as I stare down from a high cliff.
- I enjoy a large scoop of Graeter's vanilla bean ice cream on blistering hot days.

Each thing I listed is a *finite* pleasure that provides *temporary* delight. What do you delight in? What would make your list?

You sin because you get something out of it. You look at pornography or masturbate because it provides pleasure, escape, acceptance, or something else that you want. You turn to it to find satisfaction, yet God made you for something more.

King David penned Psalm 16. In it, he seeks God as his refuge and attests that no good thing comes apart from God (vv. 1–3). He expresses contentment in God's provision (vv. 4–5). The Lord provides counsel. And with God at his side, David will not be shaken (vv. 7–8). He rejoices and lives securely in God (vv. 9–10).

After listing the many evidences of God's goodness in this life, David shifts in verse 11 to the delight that comes in the life after death. God makes known to David "the path of life." This is the way that the wise often travel to find life (Prov. 6:23; 10:17; 12:28; 15:24), and it leads to God's presence, where there is "fullness of joy." Not temporary or earthly or incomplete or lesser joy. This is *fullness* of joy—a delight in God that is as good as it gets. We don't have it now, but when we stand in the presence of God, we'll experience a rich, overflowing joy that goes beyond our finite comprehension.

This is what you are made for: a fullness of joy that comes in God's presence. Does that sound good to you?

The cross makes possible this unadulterated, God-exalting joy. Commit yourself to Christ. This side of glory, we experience joy as Christians; and, as we grow in faith, joy grows as a fruit of the Spirit.

Pornography and masturbation give temporary pleasures that fill you for a moment—but, like cotton candy, the sugar high sends you crashing down a short while later. God, however, promises that at his right hand there are eternal pleasures that await you (Ps. 16:11).

Do you want fullness of joy and eternal pleasures? Doesn't that sound better to you than a life mired in pornography and masturbation?

Reflect: No matter how bad your sin problem is, abundant joy is possible for you through Christ.

Reflect: Joy trumps lust and pleasure.

Act: Pray to God and ask for more joy through Christ.

DAY 7

Slay the Beast

*For the desires of the flesh are against the Spirit, and the
desires of the Spirit are against the flesh, for these are opposed to
each other, to keep you from doing the things you want to do. . . .
Those who belong to Christ Jesus have crucified the flesh
with its passions and desires. (Gal. 5:17, 24)*

PICTURE YOURSELF AS a valiant knight—sword of the Spirit
in your sheath, shield in hand with the cross as its emblem, belt of
truth around your waist, and breastplate of righteousness on your
chest. You are ready to do battle with your mortal enemy.

Across from you is a fire-breathing, fifty-foot dragon. Almond
eyes, smoke billowing from its nostrils, spines from head to tail,
fanlike wings, and sharp teeth. It stares at you. Drool drips from
its mouth. This dragon is your sinful nature. It's your flesh.

The stark reality of this battle is that if you don't kill sin, it
will kill you. The dragon lunges at you. You hold up your shield
and swing your sword with all your strength. You fight; it attacks.
You protect yourself and then go on the offensive. The dragon
steps back, but only temporarily. You are both constantly bat-
tling each other.

Whenever you look at pornography, it's like you are throwing
this beast a juicy steak. The more you give it, the more it grows.
And it always wants more. It's *never* satisfied. The only way to
destroy its power is to starve it to death.

Your flesh and the Spirit in you are in hand-to-hand combat
with each other. The desires of the flesh are *against* the Spirit, and
the desires of the Spirit are *against* the flesh. Some days the flesh
keeps you from doing what you want to do. Some days Christians
are victorious; other days we struggle against the flesh.

Your sinful nature has its own passions and desires. "Look at another naked image." "Don't trust God." "Give in to your sin; you deserve it." "Enjoy your lust." "You need more sexual satisfaction." But when you swing that sword at the neck of the dragon, the Spirit is proclaiming, "No! Don't give in to this! Give your life to Christ, not to your sexual sin."

Your goal is simple: to put your sin to death.[1] Kill the dragon. Crucify the flesh with its passions and desires. Christ calls on you to fight the sin that dwells within you every day of your Christian life.

Don't be discouraged. In Jesus, you have everything you need for this battle.

Faith in Christ is essential to killing sin. Trust in Christ's finished work for you. Find sweet solace in your Savior. By the grace of God, if you choose faith and persist in killing the sin, don't be surprised if, over time, the dragon's chokehold on your life weakens. You are starving the beast—weakening it so that it no longer rules your life.

Reflect: What is your game plan for killing the beast? If you don't have one, that's a recipe for trouble. Don't take a *defensive* posture against sin. Through the Spirit, go on the *offensive* against your sin.

Reflect: You are not fighting on your own. Christ's death has defeated the power of sin for you.

Act: Ask a godly man or woman to help you think through a specific plan for fighting sin.

DAY 8

God's Good News for You

For one will scarcely die for a righteous person—though perhaps for a good person one would dare even to die—but God shows his love for us in that while we were still sinners, Christ died for us. (Romans 5:7–8)

HAVING EXPLAINED HOW a person can be justified by faith through the atoning work of Christ (Rom. 3:21–31) and how Abraham is a chief example of receiving the promises through faith (Rom. 4), Paul sets out his main point of Romans 5: "Therefore, since we have been justified by faith, we have peace with God through our Lord Jesus Christ" (v. 1). Those who were once ungodly (v. 6), and God's enemies (v. 10), now have access by faith to God's grace and will rejoice in the hope of the glory of God (v. 2). But, more than that, these believers will rejoice in trials that this world brings, because suffering produces perseverance, perseverance produces hope, and hope does not disappoint (vv. 3–5). God's love was poured out into their hearts through the Holy Spirit, who was given to them when they were born again (v. 5). They had no ability to change themselves or deal with their sin problem on their own, so just at the right time, Christ came into the world to die for the ungodly, like you and me (v. 6).

We're not typically going to sacrifice our life for righteous people—people who obey God's law and are upright in behavior. More likely, we would die for a good person—someone who has shown kindness to us so that we feel some obligation to reciprocate (v. 7).[1]

The apostle Paul then offers the two very important words "But God . . ." (v. 8). God is different from us. His love is much greater than our paltry unwillingness to die for anyone else. God, in giving up his Son (v. 10), showed his superior love for us. The greatest demonstration of God's love is at the cross, where Christ died for us (v. 8). One Bible translation uses a stronger word than *shows*: "Christ died for us while we were still sinners, and that is God's *proof* of his love toward us" (REB).

Just take that in for a moment: God loved you, so he sent his only Son to die *for you*. Shocking, isn't it? The King of the Universe's love is real, as is plainly evident through Christ's death, and it's *for you*.

You might wrestle with the thought, *I'm struggling with sexual sin. Is this really for me?* Yes, it is. Or you might think, *No one can love me. I'm beyond God's grace.* No, you are not. Christ's death is for sinners (v. 8), the ungodly (v. 6), God's enemies (v. 10), and the weak and powerless (v. 6). He died for those who disobeyed, missed the mark, rebelled, and ran away from God. He died for the foolish, proud, and selfish. He died *for you*.

No matter what your struggle is right now, if you repent of your sins and trust in Christ, your sin is nailed to the cross. That's good news—really the *best* news that I have to offer you.

Reflect: Relish this thought: God's love is proven in that he sent his Son to die for sinners like you. Don't rush. Meditate on it for a while.

Reflect: What things get in the way of you fully putting your trust in Christ's death for you?

Act: Talk, think, pray, and sing about Christ's death for you. The more you dwell on this fact, the more it can nourish your parched soul.

DAY 9

Isolation

*Whoever isolates himself seeks his own desire; he breaks
out against all sound judgment. (Prov. 18:1)*

SHAKESPEARE'S KING RICHARD was told that he was
born with teeth in his mouth. He responded, "And so I was, which
plainly signified that I should snarl, and bite, and play the dog.
. . . I have no brother, I am like no brother, and this word Love,
which graybeards call divine, be resident in men like one another,
and not in me; I am myself alone."[1] King Richard was a brute who
cherished isolation and scorned brotherly kindness and love.

Another king, Solomon, warned in Proverbs 18:1 that people
who deliberately isolate themselves focus on their own desires.
As you feed sexual desire, your selfish desires grow, and they
become the centerpiece of your life. One consequence of this is
a tendency to isolate yourself. Selfishness naturally separates you
from community and, even worse, makes you unfriendly to those
who should matter the most.

But it gets worse. Unfriendliness and unreasonableness go
hand in hand.[2] The one who isolates himself rages against wisdom. The sound judgment that leads him down safe paths is
abandoned or, even worse, mocked. The wisdom that is available
in a few godly friends, or even more so in a local church community, is ignored or discarded.

Isolation can kill a person's soul. Be careful of how your pornography struggles can pull you away from the very thing you
need: God's wisdom available through God's people.

God's glory and wisdom are made known through his church.
Those who follow Christ should never be isolated. A church is a
group of believers who together become a beacon of light to the

world (Eph. 3:10). Churches are salvation cooperatives, in which Christians link arms with one another and journey to heaven together.

Has your pornography habit caused you to pull away from God's people rather than to run to them? Christ died to save us from our selfish desires (2 Cor. 5:15) and to bring us into the family of God (Rom. 8:14–17; Gal. 4:6–7). For those who have faith, isolation is no longer an option.

Reflect: If you are not part of a church, is there a gospel-preaching church in your community that you can begin attending this week?

Reflect: If you are part of a church, how known are you by others in your church? If you are just attending and are not very connected, notice how isolated you are. You can faithfully go to church every week and still feel very alone. What can you do to become more deeply connected to people in your church?

Reflect: How much have you discarded wisdom that is available to you? Think about advice that some thoughtful, mature Christian gave to you in the past few months, and be critical of yourself. What excuses did you make to *not* follow this counsel? What could you to do right now to embrace the advice?

Act: The Evil One wants to destroy your life by isolating you. If you are not a member of a gospel-preaching, Jesus-loving, Bible-teaching church, then join one for the sake of your own soul.

DAY 10

Confession Is Good
for Your Soul

*Whoever conceals their sins does not prosper, but the one who
confesses and renounces them finds mercy. (Prov. 28:13 NIV)*

HAVE YOU EVER played hide-and-go-seek? It's probably been
a while since you dashed through the yard, found a spot behind
a tree, and listened to your younger sister shout, "Eighteen, nine-
teen, twenty.... Ready or not, here I come!"

In real life, we all hide. We have our reasons. There's fear.
Shame. Self-hatred. Anger. Confusion. Disappointment. Sadness.
Pride. Stubbornness. Refusing to give sin up. Greedy desires for
pleasure. But none of these are *good* reasons. The author of Proverbs warns that whoever conceals his sin does not prosper. Life
won't go well for him.

It didn't work for Adam and Eve, did it? God warned them:
"Take anything you want; just not from *that* tree." The Serpent
contradicted God: "God knows that if you eat you will be like
him. So don't listen to God." They believed the Serpent instead
of God. Guilt and shame rushed in. Adam's and Eve's eyes were
opened. "We're naked. Cover up. This is embarrassing." Then the
King's footsteps. "Oh, no—hide! Don't let him see us."

God called out to Adam: "Where are you?" And Adam cow-
ardly responded, "I heard you in the garden, and I was afraid
because I was naked, so I hid."

Really? Hide from God? Doesn't that seem ridiculous? After
all, he sees everything. He knows everything. Why did Adam and
Eve run and conceal their sin? They were afraid of being exposed.
They were ashamed of their nakedness.

33

So also with us. We don't want to be naked before God or others. Letting others see our sin is painful and embarrassing. We cover up, conceal, hide, and run away.

Confess your sin. The old adage goes: confession is good for the soul. Have you confessed your sin before God (Ps. 51:3–4) and to close friends (James 5:16)? If not, what stops you? The poor in spirit and the humble (Matt. 5:3, 5) confess their sin. Are you willing to do the same?

Renounce your sin. Say to it, "I disown you. I hate you. I don't want you. Get out of my life." Reject, discard, and turn your back on your sin.

For those who confess and renounce their sin, here's God's sweet promise: mercy awaits you at the foot of the cross.

Reflect: Think about the last time you hid your sin. What were the reasons you covered up your sin? Did hiding it benefit you?

Reflect: When's the last time you confessed your sin to God or another Christian? What stops you from confessing and rejecting your sin?

Act: Adopt the five-minute rule. Get into the habit of confessing sin *immediately* and *quickly*. Anytime you look at pornography, commit to texting, emailing, or calling another Christian right away.

DAY 11

Good Accountability

*Wisdom is the focus of the discerning, but the fool's eyes roam
to the ends of the earth. (Prov. 17:24, author's translation)*

WISDOM IS THE skill of living a godly life. It's not just knowledge about God and his Word; it involves faithfully applying it to everyday life.

The discerning make wisdom their focus. They know it is better than gold or fine jewels (Prov. 8:11; 16:16). Contrast that with the fool, whose eyes roam to the ends of the earth. The fool has no purpose, no focus, and no goals. He wanders through life without clear direction or wisdom to guide him.

If you struggle with porn, you desperately need wisdom, regardless of how aware you are of that need. You are not meant to fight this problem on your own. We all need help. Accountability is crucial to our fight for survival. Faith is not an isolated pursuit. It's relationally driven.

Good accountability is honest, frequent, local, and tough.

Honest conversations are vital. Without honesty, everything else is a waste of time. If you are not sharing the entire truth or, even worse, are lying, you undermine your friend's ability to help. For accountability to work, you've got to be brutally honest. Go to a godly, trustworthy friend and take a risk. Give him or her the nitty-gritty, ugly details of your life. Let this friend see the foulest parts of your heart. Your sin naturally pushes against this, wanting to conceal or deny, but redemption beckons you to be truthful in all your ways. "An honest answer is like a kiss on the lips" (Prov. 24:26 NIV). Like a kiss, honesty is delightful.

Frequent help is better than infrequent help. Sin daily finds ways to muck up your life. You need the repeated assistance of others pressing in on your sin in order to slow it down and prevent the mess.

Local accountability is much more useful than distant. Often I've asked a man or woman, "Who is your accountability partner?" They'll respond, "So-and-so, who is a good friend from a few years ago, when I lived in a different part of the country, still checks on me." This is not ideal. God has designed relationships such that the most powerful way to give and receive accountability is through someone who is regularly involved in your life.[1] Look for someone who goes to your church. Sit across the table from him. Sit next to her in church. Go out to lunch with him. Go for a run with her. Give him a hug. Laugh together. Search the Scriptures and pray together. All this is possible because you live geographically close to each other.

Tough conversations are intrusive. Accountability serves you well if your friend presses into your life and roots out your sin. Make sure you find someone who will ask hard, awkward, and direct questions. "Did you masturbate this week?" "Did you lie to anyone this week?" "Is there anything you are hiding from me?"

Wisdom will grow through this type of accountability. If you don't have it in your life, seek it out today.

Reflect: Does your accountability partner measure up to these four qualities: honest, frequent, local, and tough? If not, what needs to change?

Reflect: Maybe you don't have any accountability. Can you ask someone to be your accountability partner?

Act: What else do you need from your accountability partner? List what you need and then discuss the list with your accountability partner. Remember that this person can't be the Holy Spirit for you, so whatever qualities you list must be doable for him or her.

DAY 12

Bad Accountability

*Whoever walks with the wise becomes wise, but the
companion of fools will suffer harm. (Prov. 13:20)*

KING SOLOMON EXPLAINS, "Take heed to the company
you keep." If you walk with wise people, you will become wise.
If you spend time with fools, their foolishness will hurt you—or,
even worse, you too will become a fool. The company you keep
will rub off on you. What effect are your companions having on
you? Your friends, your fellow church members, and even your
accountability partner will either help or hurt.

Are you bearing good fruit because of your accountability?
What kind of accountability hurts rather than helps? Bad accountability is immature, narrow-minded, inconsistent, unreliable,
graceless, and faithless.

Immaturity is marked by a lack of wisdom. The apostle Paul
describes the spiritually immature, who are worldly in their thinking, as infants—drinking milk instead of eating solid food (1 Cor.
3:1–3; 14:20). All too often a single person finds another single
person who is fighting against sexual sin, or a married person
finds another married person who also struggles. Your friend will
understand what you're going through (after all, he or she struggles with the same problem!) but likely won't have the aggressive
disposition needed to help you fend off your sin (Matt. 5:27–30).
Why not find someone who is known to be loving, wise, and
faithful? Someone who is a season or two ahead of you in life?
Don't be surprised if such a person's life experience and study of
the Word make his or her well of wisdom much deeper.

Narrow-minded help restricts conversations to pornography. But accountability must be placed in a larger framework of

Christian friendship. It quickly becomes static if it is built solely on checking on porn struggles. You want help fighting your lust, but you need much more: hope for daily struggles, vulnerable relationships with godly men or women, and instruction on applying the gospel to different aspects of life. Accountability for sexual sin is just one component of growing in Christ.

Inconsistent and *unreliable* accountability shows up occasionally but not often enough. You need help that is frequent, reliable, and consistent.

Graceless accountability is harsh and demanding. It evokes the law often and sees little of God's grace.[1] God is the final judge, and he has already forgiven you in Christ. If your accountability partner acts like he or she is the ultimate judge, consider switching to someone else.[2]

Faithless help is dangerous for your soul. You can spend a lot of time focused on the horizontal dimensions of your life—building friendships, exercising and eating well, working hard at your job, helping your neighbor—and lose sight of the vertical. Don't lose sight of faith. Faith in Christ is the chief goal.

Reflect: Compare your accountability partner to these five criteria: immaturity, narrow-mindedness, inconsistency and unreliability, gracelessness, and faithlessness.

Reflect: If you are still not sure whether your accountability partner is mature, read over the requirements for elders and deacons in the Pastoral Epistles (1 Tim. 3; Titus 1). These form a list of maturity markers for a Christian. Though no one is sinless, what you want is someone who is *more* mature than you are rather than *less* mature. Who would that person be in your life?

Act: Always keep the gospel in clear view. For every sin struggle you talk over in your accountability conversations, be sure to talk also about the gospel. Don't assume knowledge of the gospel. Even verbalizing the gospel nourishes your soul.

DAY 13

Lying to Yourself

The getting of treasures by a lying tongue is a fleeting
vapor and a snare of death. (Prov. 21:6)

IN PROVERBS 21:6, Solomon warns that believing your lies and living by them is temporarily satisfying but, in the end, meaningless. It's like fleeting vapor. For a moment the vapor exists, and then it is gone. For a moment your lust is satisfied, but then guilt and shame rush in and take over. Solomon also says that choosing to lie to yourself is like pursuing death. The self-centered desire leads to lying, and a life committed to lying can end in literal and spiritual death (James 1:15).

Lying to satisfy your selfish desires is wrong. It's an "abomination" to God (Prov. 12:22).

To stay stuck in your sin, you lie to yourself, justify your sinful actions, or rationalize your selfish desires. Consider these typical lies of a believer struggling with pornography and masturbation:

- If God really wants me to stop, he'll give me strength.
- I can control it.
- I'll do it just one more time.
- Pornography hurts no one but me.
- I need this.
- I'm single, and I'll stop after marriage.
- If my life were better, I wouldn't be tempted to do this.
- Everyone is doing it.
- No one is watching. No one will ever know.
- God will forgive, so it doesn't matter.
- I'm stuck and nothing is going to change.
- There are no consequences, so who cares?

Lying's main purpose is to allow you to continue to sin. You lie, rationalize, or self-justify so that you can hold on to your sin. You don't want to give it up or let it go.

Did you know that Satan is the father of lies? Jesus says, "There is no truth in [Satan]. When he lies, he speaks his native language, for he is a liar and the father of lies" (John 8:44 NIV). Satan hates the truth and loves to lie.

The Scriptures tell us that God is truth. In John 17:3, Jesus says to his Father, "And this is eternal life, that they know you the only true God." The author of Hebrews says it is impossible for God to lie (Heb. 6:18). Jesus himself repeatedly says, "Truly, truly, I say to you." God himself is truth, and his words are both true in themselves and the final standard of truth. Proverbs 30:5 says, "Every word of God proves true." In God there is only truth and no sin at all.

As Christians we should not lie because we follow a God who is completely and perfectly truthful. Because God is true, we should be truth tellers. Stop lying to yourself. Every time you lie, you declare your temporary allegiance with Satan.[1] Shocking, isn't it? Believers step out of the kingdom of light and walk over to Satan's side.

Who is your master: God or Satan? Whose side are you on?

Reflect: Meditate on this verse: *"Lying lips are an abomination to the Lord, but those who act faithfully are his delight"* (*Prov. 12:22*). If lying is vile to God, why isn't it vile to you?

Reflect: Do you recognize any of the lies listed above? If so, underline them.

Act: Write out, on a sheet of paper, your lies and a biblical response to each lie.

DAY 14

A Decimated Conscience

How much more, then, will the blood of Christ, who
through the eternal Spirit offered himself unblemished to God,
cleanse our consciences from acts that lead to death, so that
we may serve the living God! (Heb. 9:14 NIV)

HAVE YOU EVER thought about what happens to your conscience when you consume pornography? Picture your conscience as a circle. A clear line divides good from evil, right from wrong.

After repeated exposure to porn, the line in your conscience becomes fuzzy and less distinct.

The first time you look at porn, your alarm bells go off. Your conscience says, "Don't do this. It's exciting, but it's wrong." But after time, with repeated exposure, the alarm bells grow silent. If you are entrenched in porn, the length of time between having a sexual thought and acting it out becomes shorter. Recurrent exposures have numbed your conscience, and the line between right and wrong is blurred. Your carnal desires begin to rule your heart as you continue to feed the pornography habit. Your conscience dies, and your selfish desires take over your life—a deadly combination.

What revives your conscience? No medicine or generic system of redemption fixes this. You need a Savior who is willing to shed his blood for you. Christ, the unblemished sacrifice, offered himself so that your inner person can be renewed and your defiled conscience restored.

Have you ever had a dirty feeling after you've looked at pornography? In the Old Testament sacrificial system, an animal's life was given to externally purify those who were dirty, defiled, and unclean. The blood of goats and bulls and the ashes of a heifer temporarily made the impure outwardly clean (Heb. 9:13). But these sacrifices didn't offer lasting, internal transformation. Prior to Jesus's life and death, people had to repeatedly offer sacrifices to deal with their sin. But Christ gave himself as a one-time sacrifice for us (Heb. 9:12, 14). How much more valuable is the blood of Jesus than any animal! Jesus's sacrifice rendered an internal change in your life, cleansing your defiled conscience from sexual sins that lead to death.

As you trust in Christ's sacrifice, the Holy Spirit quickens your conscience (Rom. 9:1; Heb. 9:14). God's supernatural power revives the ethical line in your conscience, making it more distinct again.

What's your part in all this? Repentance and obedience. Every act of repentance and every small step of obedience reclaims your conscience a bit at a time and puts to death your selfish desires (Gal. 5:24). A thousand small steps of obedience rebuild your character. Repentance and obedience truly matter.

Reflect: Do you know how crucial Christ's atonement is for your battle against pornography? Look at a few atonement texts to enrich your soul: Isaiah 53:3–6; Mark 10:43–45; Romans 3:23–26; 5:6–11; 8:32–39; 2 Corinthians 5:21.

Reflect: Obedience matters. Are there things you *should* be doing that you are *not* doing yet?

Act: Memorize the gospel. Pick an atonement text (listed above) and commit it to memory. Turn it over again and again in your heart and mind. Squeeze everything you can out of this text. Let it nourish and refresh your soul.

DAY 15

Go to War on Your Doubts

*See to it, brothers and sisters, that none of you has a sinful, unbelieving
heart that turns away from the living God. But encourage one
another daily . . . so that none of you may be hardened by sin's
deceitfulness. We have come to share in Christ, if indeed we hold our
original conviction firmly to the very end. (Heb. 3:12–14 NIV)*

AFTER SPEAKING ABOUT faithful Moses (Heb. 3:1–6), and
reminding his readers of Israel's disobedience and unbelief (vv.
7–11), the author of Hebrews warns his readers (Jewish Christians—and also you!) not to follow Israel's negative example.
Take care that you don't let unbelief corrupt your heart. As you
struggle with pornography, do you doubt God's power to change
you? Or do you doubt that there is a living God?

Much like the Israelites, who rebelled and whose hearts went
astray (Heb. 3:8, 10), or the fool who says, "There is no God" (Ps.
14:1), you probably wrestle with doubt. Especially on days when
you give in to temptation, it's all too easy to think things like:

- Maybe God isn't good after all.
- Maybe God is good, but he's not good to me.
- God doesn't care. He doesn't love me.
- God won't fulfill his promises to me.
- Christ's death is insufficient.
- Christ's mercy doesn't extend to me.
- Christ can never forgive me; I'm too far gone.
- Maybe my faith just doesn't matter anymore.

Do any of these ring true for you? If sexual sin rules your
life, doubts will stack up. The seeds of unbelief take root in your
hardening heart. The author of Hebrews warns you to not give

yourself over to your unbelief, lest you fall away from the living God (Heb. 3:12). For the Jewish Christians, this meant returning to Judaism and abandoning Christ. Where does doubt lead you?

What can you do about the doubts that plague your life? You can't fight doubt on your own. You need daily encouragement from other believers (Heb. 3:13). You need a community of Christians who will tell you what is true, refute your doubts, and point you to the cross. In the kingdom of Christ, no one has to fight alone. Daily grace awaits you as you war with your doubts.

Are you waiting around until others help you? Stop it! Here's your responsibility: to hold firmly to the end your original convictions about the gospel (Heb. 3:14). Faith in Christ matters. True Christians will persevere.

You might doubt whether you will make it. There might be days when you think, *What's the use of fighting this anymore?* Sin is deceitful. Just as it tricked Adam and Eve in the garden (Gen. 3), so also it will mislead you and harden your heart (Heb. 3:13). Don't give in to unbelief. Humbly ask Christian friends or mentors for help, cast away your doubts, and trust that God can redeem your life through Christ.

Reflect: What bad fruit of unbelief shows up in your life? Have you isolated yourself? Are you struggling to trust God's character and power? Have you grown agitated, frustrated, angry, sad, or fearful? Have you stopped going to church, reading the Word, or praying?

Reflect: If you have reached the point where your heart is hardened toward God, don't give up. Plead with God for mercy.

Act: Write out your doubts, and begin to pray through them. Your prayers can be simple: "God, I'm struggling to trust your goodness. Please help me."

DAY 16

Forgiveness in Christ

When you were dead in your sins . . . God made you alive with Christ. He forgave us all our sins, having canceled the charge of our legal indebtedness, which stood against us and condemned us; he has taken it away, nailing it to the cross. (Col. 2:13–14 NIV)

YOU SIGN AN IOU promising God *perfect* obedience. He takes the note, seals it, and hands it back to you. You then go and live your life, but your flesh (your natural disposition to sin) causes problems. You look at pornography. You masturbate. You have sexual thoughts. Plus you pile on other typical sins: pride, anger, a loose tongue, and selfishness. You owe God perfect obedience, but you fail.[1]

Satan takes the IOU and goes back to God, who sits high on the judge's bench. Wagging his finger at you, Satan bellows, "You failed to honor your promise!" He waves the IOU back and forth for dramatic effect. "You owed God perfect obedience, and what did you do? You committed sexual sin again! And again! And again! You now owe us your life because of your disobedience."

God the judge says, "The prosecutor has brought a charge of death against you." He pauses and looks right into your eyes. "Death is an appropriate penalty for your disobedience." God slams the gavel down on his desk. "I hereby sentence you to physical and spiritual death!" The foreman walks over to you and puts you in handcuffs and chains. The weight of your sin bears down on you. You know you deserve this punishment.

But the story doesn't end there. Jesus enters through the back door of the courtroom, walks up, and stands right next to Satan. He reaches out his hand and waits. Satan looks at Jesus, looks at you, and is infuriated. He barks at Jesus, "No!" Yet Jesus, perfectly calm, waits, his hand still held out. Like a volcano that's spitting out burning lava, Satan screams and then, begrudgingly, hands over the note.

Jesus walks past the judge and keeps going until he reaches Calvary. He nails your IOU to the cross and climbs onto it himself. Roman soldiers send nails through his hands and feet. Blood is shed. It's a gruesome death—one that no innocent man should ever go through.

And your IOU is wiped clean. Your debt is cancelled, paid for by his death. Only the perfectly obedient God-Man is worthy to be a perfect sacrifice for you. His death means that you no longer have to die. Instead of death, you are given life through Christ.

In the courtroom, God turns to you, looking you in the eye again, and says, "Because of Christ's death, you are forgiven of all your sin. You are free to go." Immediately, the handcuffs and chains fall off. Tears well up in your eyes. *How could Christ do this for me,* you think, *especially after all I've done to fail him?* The answer is simple but profound: he did it because he loves you.

> **Reflect:** The third stanza of Horatio Spafford's beautiful hymn "It is Well with My Soul" captures the point well:
>
> > My sin—O the bliss of this glorious thought!—
> > My sin, not in part, but the whole,
> > Is nailed to the cross and I bear it no more;
> > Praise the Lord, praise the Lord, O my soul![2]
>
> **Reflect:** Isn't it remarkable that *all* your sins have been paid for?
>
> **Act:** Write out a brief prayer thanking God for your forgiveness in Christ.

DAY 17

Come out of the Darkness
and into the Light

At one time you were darkness, but now you are light in the Lord.
Walk as children of light (for the fruit of light is found in all that is
good and right and true).... Take no part in the unfruitful works
of darkness, but instead expose them.... But when anything
is exposed by the light, it becomes visible, for anything that
becomes visible is light. (Eph. 5:8–9, 11, 13–14)

IN THE BIBLE, darkness is associated with an immoral, sinful life apart from God. Light describes purity, truth, and holiness. In Ephesians 5, Paul doesn't say, "For at one time you were *in* the darkness," but "For at one time you *were* darkness." You were not *surrounded* by darkness. You *were* darkness. Sin defined you. This is who you were prior to your life in Christ.

But now you are light in the Lord. Just as you *were* darkness, now that you've given your life to Christ, you *are* light. Christ rules you, not sin. The gospel, not your sin, now defines you. The term *walk* is used to indicate the manner in which you live your Christian life. If you are light, you are to live as a child of the light. If you know the truth about Jesus (Eph. 4:20–21), what you know and believe should be demonstrated in how you live. The fruit of the light is all that is good and right and true.

If life in Christ is fruitful, then a sinful life is fruitless. The deeds done in the darkness don't yield good for your life. You experience temporary guilty pleasures, but they just leave you hungering for more.

The disobedient are those who are sexually immoral, impure, greedy, obscene, and foolish in their speech (Eph. 5:3–7). Here's the apostle's warning: Don't share in the sins of the disobedient.

Take no part in these unfruitful works of the darkness; instead, expose them with the light of Christ. Darkness and light are in opposition. If you've given your life to Christ, you are light. You should no longer pursue immoral acts, but instead, as light, you should expose your sexual sin. Drag your sin, kicking and screaming, out of the darkness and demand an answer. Let evil be shown for what it really is. Bring your sin to the light of Christ.

How many times have you looked at pornography behind a closed door? How many times have you masturbated in the shower? How many times have you looked at naked images in secrecy? These things that are done in secret are so abhorrent it is shameful to even talk about them (Eph. 5:12). Let the light of Christ shine on the darkness. Stop struggling in the darkness on your own.

Anything exposed by the light becomes visible. Darkness can't stay dark when light is shining in it. It is transformed into light. Your evil deeds are put to death (Gal. 5:24), and your life is changed, by the light of Christ (Eph. 2:1–10; 5:14).

You are light in Christ. You might doubt that right now, but it's true. So, as light, don't tolerate the darkness and sin in your life. Let the light of Christ shine on your sinful deeds. Live as you were made to live: as a child of the light.

> **Reflect:** Read John 3:19–21. Ask yourself: Do I hate the light? Do I fear my deeds being exposed? Or am I living by the truth, and have I come into Christ's light?
>
> **Reflect:** Are you afraid to bring your dark deeds into the light? What is most scary about it? Is shame getting in the way?
>
> **Act:** Pray for Christ's light to shine on your sin.

DAY 18

Building Relationships

A man of many companions may come to ruin, but there is a friend who sticks closer than a brother. (Prov. 18:24)

MATT COMPLAINED TO me, "I'm having trouble getting other men to talk to me about what's really going on in their lives. We can talk about sports or their job, but if I try to go deeper I run into walls." Matt is not alone. I've often talked with men and women who feel like they lack depth in relationships. They feel alone because no one is close enough to know the depth of their pain and struggles.

Most people show up on a Sunday morning and do a good job of putting on a happy face. Christians are great at putting masks on. You ask, "How are you?" Your friend responds (almost automatically), "Fine—how are you?" But what if your friend dropped the mask and said, "I'm struggling in my job, my headaches are not going away, and I'm wrestling with doubt. It's been a hard week." You'd be shocked, wouldn't you? You probably wouldn't know what to do with such brutal honesty.

In Proverbs 18:24, King Solomon says that a man can have many companions but still come to ruin. The quantity of your friends matters little if you don't have someone who will stick with you during adversity. Consider the commitment that biological relatives show to one another. As the cliché goes, "Blood is thicker than water." Now imagine a friend who is even more loyal than a blood brother. This is the quality of friendship that Solomon commends.

This type of important friendship includes *depth*; the friend "sticks closer than a brother." If a brother is devoted to you, how much greater is this friend's commitment! If a brother is honest with you, how much greater is this friend's transparency! If a brother is loving, how much greater is the kindness of your friend!

This friendship also includes *perseverance*; the friend sticks with you through adversity. A brother may live far away, so who is going to help you during your time of trouble? A friend who is near (Prov. 27:10).

The sweetness of this kind of friendship is better than worldly luxury or good advice (Prov. 27:9). Having a few quality friendships is more valuable than an abundance of shallow relationships. What matters is not *quantity* but *quality* of your friendships.

Of course, the greatest of all friends is Christ. Astonishingly, Christ, who is our Redeemer and Lord, called us friends (John 15:12–15). As Christ said, the greatest act of love is to give up your life for your friends. That's exactly what Christ did for sinners.

Reflect: How are you doing in your relationship with Christ? Jesus said that if you keep his commands, you will remain in his love and be his friend (John 15:10, 14). In what ways do you need to grow in your obedience to God's Word so that you can be close to Christ and fruitful for his kingdom (John 15:16)?

Reflect: While it is easy to criticize others, the best way to build relationships with greater depth and perseverance is by examining yourself first. How are you doing in being devoted, honest, and loving with your friends?

Act: Can you think of at least one friendship in which you can take practical steps to grow the relationship? Two ideas: (1) One person showing humility often engenders humility in others, so take your mask off, share honestly with a friend, and see what happens. (2) Show a deliberate act of kindness to a friend. Not something simple or easy—do something that is personally costly to you and hugely beneficial to your friend.

DAY 19

Take Hold of God's Promise

I am sure of this, that he who began a good work in you will
bring it to completion at the day of Jesus Christ. (Phil. 1:6)

WHEN YOU FALL into pornography, your sin feels big and God seems small. You wrestle with guilt and shame. You're frustrated with yourself and feel distant from God. You fight to return to a place where God is again a big God. Your kingdom of self should never be bigger than God's kingdom.

Every time he remembered the Christians in Philippi, Paul was thankful (Phil. 1:3). He prayed for them with joy because of their partnership in the gospel (vv. 4–5). He had great confidence—not in himself, and not in the Philippian Christians, but in God. God began "a good work" in them, and he would "bring it to completion" when Christ returned (v. 6). This "good work" was the salvation that God wrought in these believers, who were learning with "fear and trembling" to work out their salvation (Phil. 2:12) in the context of Christian community.

How appropriate. Paul had immense confidence that God would finish what he started. God doesn't save you and then leave you on your own to battle sexual sin. He will bring your sanctification to completion. This is a *certain* promise because God is making it. When you feel stuck in your sin, do you turn to this promise and believe in the one who has offered it to you?

Don't let your feelings about your sin dictate what you think God is doing. God will make you just like his Son. "We know that when [Jesus] appears we will be like him, because we shall see him as he is" (1 John 3:2). Some days this will feel impossible—or, at the most, a remote possibility. But the promise of Philippians 1:6 is sure, and your responsibility is to take hold of this promise by faith.

Don't let your vision be reduced to the scope of your sexual sin. Lift your eyes and look beyond your sin to the long-term work that God is doing in you. Some seasons you will descend into valleys of disappointment and self-inflicted difficulties. Other days you'll make progress, grow in faith, and be encouraged. Your spiritual progress may be a roller coaster, but that doesn't deny the certainty of the end result. Your confidence is in God and not in you.

What if I showed you the end of time, when Jesus comes back? You'd be deeply encouraged to know that it all works out in the end. You'd see God's promises fulfilled. You'd know that God's Word is true. Now return to the present day. Why not look forward to Christ's return with that same certainty? Why not trust that God will honor his promises?

Sometimes it helps to step back for a long-term view of your sanctification. Where were you when the problem started? Where are you now? It's easy to be overly focused on your struggle with sexual sin right now. You think all about one tree while losing sight of the forest. Step back and look at everything there is to see—the many trees, flowers, grass, and bushes. Don't lose sight of what God is doing with your life and who you will be when Christ returns.

Reflect: How confident are you that God will do what he says?

Reflect: In what ways has God already been working in your life to fight sexual sin? Have you thanked him for it?

Act: Find a mature believer and talk about what your sexual sins looked like when the trouble started, where you are today, and where you hope you will be in five or ten years from now.

DAY 20

Guard Your Heart

Keep your heart with all vigilance, for from it
flow the springs of life. (Prov. 4:23)

DAVID TEXTED ME, "I've fallen again." After a rough week, Jane told her best friend, "I'm struggling and don't know what to do." How should David and Jane guard their lives from the onslaught of sexual images, videos, and chat rooms they face? How should you?

Consider Proverbs 4. A father asks his son to heed his words of advice, "for they are life to those who find them and health to one's whole body" (Prov. 4:20–22 NIV). He passes on wisdom and warns his son about the ravages of sexual immorality (Prov. 5–7). The son should keep his mouth from perversity and corrupt talk and should keep his eyes and feet fixed on the godly path (Prov. 4:24–26). He must avoid evil and choose good (Prov. 4:27). But, above all else, the son is to guard his heart (v. 23). Remember that from your heart flow the springs of life (v. 23). Your heart sustains your life, just as a spring of water sustains life in a dry desert.

What practical steps have you taken to guard your heart?

Do you have an internet filter program on all your electronic devices? Programs like Covenant Eyes help Christians who are struggling by exposing what they are viewing online to an accountability partner.

Are you aggressive in cutting off access points to pornography? You need to cut off *every* access point (Matt. 5:27–30). Passivity leads to pornography taking over your life.

Are you willing to cut out the danger zones? These are the typical times and places in which you stumble. For example, a single man or woman may look at pornography late at night. Such strugglers could give over their devices when their roommates go to bed, or by 10 pm (whichever comes first).

Do you guard your eyes from visual temptation? It takes deliberate skill to avert your eyes from the many forms of temptation in our culture.

Do you have accountability? Or are you fighting this problem on your own? What excuses have you used to avoid seeking help? What fears are getting in the way of you seeking proper help?

Are you confessing quickly and immediately to accountability partners? Do your lies and self-justifications deceive you into thinking that you can wait before you bring your sin into the light? The quicker you confess to God and other Christians, the better it is for your soul.

Do you proactively make plans when you think you might be vulnerable? For example, if you often get bored on the weekends and stumble into pornography, do you find ways to steward your time wisely? If you are married and your spouse is away, how can you use the time wisely while he or she is gone?

If you travel, how do you protect yourself while in a hotel room alone? Can you have friends check in on you? Can you lock the television/cable remote in the hotel safe or give it to the desk? How else can you protect yourself while you are more vulnerable?

Ask God to watch over, sustain, and protect you. Plead with the Lord to give you strength. Christ died for you. His death gives you life. You can't do any of this on your own, so give your life to Christ and let him help you.

Reflect: You can't win this battle by your own strength. You need help from the Lord, the Spirit, and your church.

Reflect: What other ways do you need to guard your heart?

Act: Write out a battle plan for how you will guard your heart. Share it with a trusted friend who can hold you accountable.

DAY 21

Make No Provision for the Flesh

*Let us walk properly as in the daytime, not in orgies and drunkenness,
not in sexual immorality and sensuality, not in quarrelling and
jealousy. But put on the Lord Jesus Christ, and make no provision
for the flesh, to gratify its desires. (Rom. 13:13–14)*

GOD HAS ONLY one event left on his calendar. The pressures of
life often leave you living for the moment, the day, or the coming
week, but the apostle Paul says that you should always live with an
eye on the final day, when Christ returns (Rom. 13:11) and salvation comes to fruition. Our final deliverance is nearer to us than
when we first believed. Christians are to cast off the darkness (the
sin that entangles their lives) and protect themselves with the
armor of light (Rom. 13:12). The present evil age is almost over,
and the coming day of God's final kingdom is almost here (v. 12).

In light of this day, your conduct should honor God. You
should not participate in sexual immorality and sensuality but
rather clothe yourself with Christ (vv. 13–14). Follow his example. Grow to be like him, especially in love, kindness, compassion,
humility, peace, and patience.

As you put on the character of Christ, you are to make no
room for the evil desires of your flesh (v. 14). The flesh says, "Give
me what I want. I'm hungry!" Deny it. Starve it. Don't give in to
its reckless desires. As long as you wait for the final day, you are
not to make provision for the flesh.

What are some ways you might feed your sinful flesh? You
may look at pornography, watch videos, sext, or participate in sexually explicit chat rooms. You may seek out images of the opposite
sex, or you may want more: same-sex material, S&M (sadism and
masochism), orgies . . . the list goes on and on. Then you move

from looking to acting out. You slip into premarital sex. Or you sleep with others—maybe a prostitute—have an affair, or visit a strip club. In the shower or late at night in bed, you masturbate.

But there are other ways to make provision for the flesh. Think about websites that you visit. Sports or news sites are notorious for posting sexually revealing pictures to grab your attention. Maybe you rent a movie that you know has a sex scene in it. Rather than fast-forward through it, you watch. In spring and summer time, as clothing becomes more revealing, you let your eyes linger longer. Each passing moment feeds the flesh more.

The apostle Paul elsewhere warns, "A man reaps what he sows. Whoever sows to please their flesh, from the flesh will reap destruction" (Gal. 6:7–8 NIV). What you plant in the spring will dictate your harvest in the fall (Hos. 8:7). If you continue to feed the flesh's appetite and orient yourself around its desires, you should expect to "reap destruction." Your sinful choices will mess up your life.

If you are making provision for the flesh, choose by the power of the Holy Spirit to say no to ungodliness this very day. Plead with God to show mercy and to help you break your sinful habit.

> **Reflect:** Sexual sin leads you down a destructive path. In what ways have your pornography or masturbation struggles hurt your life?
>
> **Reflect:** What ways do you want to grow more like Christ?
>
> **Act:** What could you do today to say no to sexual sin? For example, if you have been watching sexually explicit movies, cancel your media subscription. If you have been viewing seductive ads on the sidebar of a sports website, stop going to that site or get an ad blocker.

DAY 22

The Internal War

*I appeal to you . . . by the mercies of God, to present your bodies as a
living sacrifice, holy and acceptable to God, which is your spiritual
worship. Do not be conformed to this world, but be transformed by the
renewal of your mind, that by testing you may discern what is the will
of God, what is good and acceptable and perfect. (Rom. 12:1–2)*

IN ROMANS 12, Paul transitions from his extended theological
treatise in chapters 1 through 11 to urge believers to live in light
of God's mercy. He appeals to the believers in Rome (and also to
you) to do three things.

Present your bodies as living sacrifices (v. 1). Commit your
whole self to God. Unlike Old Testament sacrifices (animals that
were killed), the children of God are a "living sacrifice." You're
alive in Christ and no longer dead in your sins.

Do not to be conformed to this world (v. 2). The world tries to
pressure you into its mold. We should, by God's strength, resist
the world.

*Be transformed by the renewing of your mind so that by testing
you can discern what is the will of God* (v. 2). The verb *transformed*
is passive, referring not to something we do but to what is done
to us. The same verb is used in Mark 9, when Jesus was "trans-
figured" before his three disciples. He became radiant, intensely
white. There was a *radical* change in his body and appearance.
When God transforms us, he effects a *fundamental* change—
starting from within, in the heart (Jer. 31:33; Ezek. 36:26) and
mind (Col. 3:2). When this happens, a believer is able to discern
God's good, perfect, and pleasing will.

In Romans 12:2, Paul focuses on the battleground of your
mind. Think about the images embedded in your brain. You can

find ways to escape external temptations, but you can't run from your mind. Sexual sin changes you. Every time you act out, you negatively conform your mind to look more like the evil in this world than like your Savior.

What hope is there for the struggler to deal with this internal damage? If you trust in Christ, *God will change you.* The Holy Spirit within you will change you over time, starting with your inner life. Daily contact with the gospel is vital, because you need a supernatural transformation. The mind changes when it's set on what the Spirit desires (Rom. 8:5). The Spirit can supernaturally clean up your brain over time, giving you the "life" and "peace" that come to a mind that is governed by the Spirit (Rom. 8:6).

Consider one example of the internal war. A lot of men and women struggle with fantasizing. It's tempting to draw on images in your mind and turn them into a movie-reel fantasy, sexually arousing yourself and sometimes finishing off with masturbation. Does this sound familiar?

As you commit your life to him, God transforms you to be more like his Son (2 Cor. 3:18). By his strength, it becomes possible for you to say no to ungodliness from within. You can resist evil. Don't settle for just fighting temptations externally. God can clean up your mind, your heart, and your inner person. Do you believe this? Do you trust that he can actually change you?

Reflect: How often do you have contact with the gospel? What can you do to make sure you have daily doses of the gospel?

Reflect: Have you settled for just fighting external temptations? Can you also fight the battlegrounds within your mind and heart? Can you discipline yourself to say no to fantasizing?

Act: Share with a godly friend how you are tempted to conform to the world, and strategize how you can live by faith instead.

DAY 23

A Warning against Pride

The highway of the upright turns aside from evil; whoever guards his way preserves his life. Pride goes before destruction, and a haughty spirit before a fall. (Prov. 16:17–18)

TOMMY STRUGGLES FOR several years with pornography. By God's grace, he resolves to fight. He finds accountability and starts using internet filter programs. He actively guards his eyes and heart. He joins a gospel-preaching church. He is in the Word personally much more and is attentive to the preached Word on Sundays. His love for God and God's people grows. Some days the temptations are fierce, but over time things start to turn around. Sexual sin loses its grip, and eventually he enjoys the tangible benefit of porn-free days.

Then the Evil One pours poison into this man's heart. A seed of pride sprouts; its roots grow and wind their way through his heart. He thinks, "I got this." He lets down his guard. His vigilance slips away, and then it happens: he gives in to the temptation to look. His pride messed him up.

In the Iron Age of Israel (1100–600 BC), a highway was the main thoroughfare for travel. These highways passed by cities, not through them. To go to a city, a person would "turn aside" from the highway (Judges 19:11–12, 15) and take an access road.[1] Proverbs 16:17 indicates that the upright (those who are humble before God[2]) travel on the highway and avoid evil. They shun the access roads to the condemned city and stay on the godly path. The upright man doesn't let down his guard once he's passed the city but maintains his vigilance.

If the upright are cautious and avoid evil (Prov. 14:16), the proverbial fool is prideful, reckless, and lacking sense (Prov. 11:2;

14:16; 17:16). Proverbs 16:18 says that pride leads to "destruction" and a haughty spirit to a "fall." Tommy's confidence was the precursor to his failure. Can you relate to Tommy's experience? Do you see how pride corrupts your life and sabotages your efforts at purity?

God opposes the proud and shows grace to the humble (James 4:6). If you are marked by pride, God is *against* your pride. Picture a father who loves his child but sees pride sending him down a destructive path. The father confronts his prideful son because he loves him but hates the mess that his sin will create. God lovingly says to you, "Repent." Nail your pride to the cross and plead with God for mercy. Through Christ, your pride can be put to death. Ask him for humility.

Reflect: Are you too dependent on yourself? Do you have a hard time asking for help? Are you unwilling to listen to reasonable advice? Are you defensive when someone points out your faults? Do you often think that you are right and others are wrong? Do you get angry at others? Do you not like admitting your faults or your weaknesses? Do you struggle to obey authority figures? If you answer yes to any of these questions, you are struggling with pride.

Reflect: If someone asked you to cut your access to the internet, to get rid of an application on your phone, to install an internet filter program on your devices, or even to dumb down your phone, how would you respond? With pride or humility?

Act: The antidote to pride is humility. Take some time to read through these texts, and pray over them, asking the Lord for humility: Mic. 6:8; Matt. 23:10–12; Phil. 2:3–4; 1 Peter 5:5–6.

DAY 24

Humility

Do nothing out of selfish ambition or vain conceit. Rather, in humility value others above yourselves, not looking to your own interests but each of you to the interests of the others. In your relationships with one another, have the same mindset as Christ Jesus. (Phil. 2:3–5 NIV)

FROM HIS PRISON cell, the apostle Paul wrote to the believers in Philippi (Phil. 1:1), encouraging them in their faith. He exhorted them to "do nothing out of selfish ambition and vain conceit." Don't live a life that's motivated by self-advancement, empty glory, and self-fulfillment. That's worldly, not Christian.

"Rather, in humility value others above yourselves." The word *above* is translated later in this letter as "surpassing" (3:8; see also 4:7). Instead of living a life that revolves around your own needs and wants, focus on the interests of others (2:4). How do you live this kind of other-centered life? Paul says, "In humility" (v. 3).

Humility is living a meek, servant-hearted life because of who God is and what he's done for us. God is glorious. If you truly know him, you will strive for his greatness and not your own.

Where does humility come from? From Christ. Because Jesus became nothing and humbled himself by becoming obedient to death on a cross (vv. 7–8), you can be humble. Even as you struggle with sexual sin, every new moment provides an opportunity for you to give yourself to Christ again, to grow closer to him, and *then* to watch him change you. The indicatives (who you are in Christ) undergird Paul's imperative (the command to be humble). As you grow in trusting Christ, humility will grow.

Sexual sin is fundamentally selfish. You look at a man or woman who doesn't belong to you. You satisfy your pleasures. You pursue what you want. In the moment of the forbidden, you are big, because life revolves around your self-fulfillment, and God is small. He doesn't matter. In fact, you forget about him as you put your interests above his.

Sexual sin prioritizes your carnal desires over people. It distorts your relationships. Image-bearers were never meant to find satisfaction through a screen. Real relationships come as you follow the golden rule—loving others as you love yourself (Mark 12:31).

Because of your life in Christ, Paul encourages you to reverse course. By God's strength, reject your selfishness and start learning to put others first. *Humility comes first through knowing Christ.* Paul's encouragement is to take on this humble mindset, which is yours in Christ (Phil. 2:5). Use your freedom in Christ to find ways to serve others in love (Gal. 5:13) rather than making provisions to satisfy your flesh.

Humility grows as you exercise it. It's a lot like a muscle. You actually grow more humble as you act on your love for others. As you love and serve someone else, you are helping not only them but also yourself as you grow to be more like Christ.

Reflect: We grow in humility because of who Christ is and what he did on the cross for us. But, as he is in everything, Christ is also the ultimate example for us of humility. Christ *"made himself nothing, taking the form of a servant,* being born in the likeness of men. And being found in human form, *he humbled himself by becoming obedient to the point of death,* even death on a cross" (Phil. 2:7–8).

Reflect: Christ "came not to be served but to serve, and to give his life as a ransom for many" (Mark 10:45). Would you follow him by serving others?

Act: Exercise humility. Find someone who needs help, find out what they need, and then do it.

DAY 25

Fighting Temptations

God is faithful, and he will not let you be tempted beyond
your ability, but with the temptation he will also provide
the way of escape, that you may be able to endure it.
Therefore, my beloved, flee from idolatry. (1 Cor. 10:13–14)

IN 1 CORINTHIANS 10, Paul uses the Israelites as a negative example to warn believers in Corinth "not [to] desire evil as
they did" (v. 6). He warns them not to be idolaters (v. 7), not
to indulge in sexual immorality (v. 8), not to put Christ to the
test (v. 9), and not to grumble (v. 10). Very few of the Israelites
had faith, and "with most of them God was not pleased" (v. 5).
Paul warns the Corinthians not to give in to their cravings for evil,
because that would lead to God's judgment, as many of the Israelites experienced. Every runner runs a race in order to make it to
the finish line and obtain the prize (1 Cor. 9:24–26), but very few
of the Israelites made it to the end.

Amid these warnings, Paul offers an encouragement (10:13).
The Israelites and Corinthians faced these temptations, and so
will you. No temptation that you face is unique to you. You are
not alone. God offers divine help. He is faithful. He has shown
himself to be so in the past, and he will continue to be so in the
future. God will not let you be tempted beyond your ability to
resist. No temptation is too much for you. By the power of the
Spirit (and not your own strength), you can say no. God will provide a way out when you face temptation, so that you will be able
to endure it. The way out is to flee the temptation, whether it is
idolatry (v. 14), sexual immorality, or another danger.

You might think, "The temptation is too strong; I can't help
it." Satan continues to tempt you (1 Thess. 3:5) and wants you to

believe that the temptation is stronger than you—that you have no choice but to give in. If you believe such nonsense, you've contradicted God. The Lord says that he can provide the strength you need to resist the temptation.

Often, as we fight temptation, we focus on the tantalizing image in front of us, not on the carnal desire raging within us. But by God's strength you can curb carnal appetites for pornography, sex, and masturbation. The power of the Spirit in you is greater than your carnal appetite. The Israelites had a choice, but some gave in to their cravings and fell in the wilderness. You have a choice also. Paul's encouragement to you is that you don't have to give in. By faith, you can choose the way of escape that God provides. The only question is: will you take it?

The author of Hebrews tells us that Jesus was "one who in every respect has been tempted as we are, yet without sin" (4:15). When you face temptation, you either give in or flee before the temptation is fully felt. Only Jesus knows the full strength of the temptation, because he never gave in.[1] The sinless one knows the power and strength of the temptation more than we do. And he will give you the strength that you need to resist. What an amazing Savior!

Reflect: Have you learned to discipline your carnal appetites?

Reflect: How do you fight temptations? Take a moment to examine your approach to fighting temptations.[2] Are you trusting in God's power to fight?

Act: Ask a few older, wiser Christians how they fight temptation and curb their carnal appetites.

DAY 26

Shame

*"You are to distinguish between . . .
the unclean and the clean." (Lev. 10:10)*

SALLY LOOKED AT images on a porn site that had often been her stumbling block. Immediately afterward, she felt filthy. She went to church but felt like she didn't belong because of what she had done.

Consider the biblical category of being *unclean.* To be unclean is to be defiled or contaminated. In the Old Testament, unclean people were separated from the clean because they contaminated the clean. They were rejected. The unclean knew that they didn't belong, so, like lepers, they stayed apart from the rest.[1] The law required them to live outside the city or town and to warn others by shouting, "Unclean! Unclean!" (Lev. 13:45–46).

Do you know what this feels like? You have a deep sense of being dirty after viewing pornography, masturbating, viewing sexually explicit videos, or engaging in premarital sex. In creating a moral universe, God established right and wrong. When you violate God's moral order, you feel the wrongness of what you've done. You can use a lot of words to describe how you feel after sinning sexually: *dirty, filthy, outcast, rejected,* or *defiled.* These all merge together into the experience we call shame.

Sally felt ashamed—embarrassed before God and others. In her case, it was a double dose. Because porn struggles are supposedly a man's problem, she felt embarrassed that as a woman she struggled in this way.

In his writing in the Old Testament, Moses distinguished between *the unclean and the clean* (Lev. 10:10). The clean is not contaminated or dirty but is pure, washed, and uninfected.

A clean man or woman feels normal, not embarrassed. They haven't touched anything impure and become filthy themselves, so they are an accepted and normal part of the community.

The pathway out of shame is not nearly as easy as taking a shower to wash away physical dirt. In the Old Testament, sacrifices were made to purify the unclean and make them clean again (Lev. 16:30). But, on this side of the cross, the unclean are made clean through Christ.

In Mark 1:40–45, a man with leprosy approached Jesus and fell on his knees, begging him, "If you are willing, you can make me clean" (v. 40 NIV). The leper had such faith that Jesus could help him that he forsook the law's requirements for the chance to see Jesus. The unclean approached the clean. It was not Jesus's ability to heal that was in question, just his willingness.

Jesus, in response, did the most shocking thing—he reached out and touched the leper. The clean touched the unclean. Religious and social regulations were no barrier for Jesus. "I am willing," Jesus said. "Be clean!" (v. 41 NIV). Immediately the leprosy left the man, and he was cleansed.

What Jesus did for the leper, he can do for you. Jesus can purify you, wash you clean, get rid of your shame, and welcome you back into the family of God. Do you believe this? Will you come to him to be cleansed?

> **Reflect:** After looking at pornography, do you wrestle with anger at yourself, feelings of guilt or shame, and distance from God? How do you deal with these things?
>
> **Reflect:** How would you describe your experience of shame?
>
> **Act:** Echo the leper's actions and plea—boldly approach Jesus and ask, "If you are willing, you can make me clean."

DAY 27

The Love of Christ

For I am sure that neither death nor life, nor angels nor rulers,
nor things present nor things to come, nor powers, nor height nor
depth, nor anything else in all creation, will be able to separate us
from the love of God in Christ Jesus our Lord. (Rom. 8:38–39)

To CONCLUDE HIS magnificent chapter, the apostle Paul asks
and answers several questions at the end of Romans 8.

> Who can be against us?
> *No one, because God is for us (v. 31).*
> Will God not graciously give us all things?
> *He who already gave his Son for us all will also graciously give*
> *us all things (v. 32).*
> Who will bring a charge against God's elect?
> *No one, because God has justified us (v. 33).*
> Who will condemn us?
> *No one, because Christ died and was raised by God and is at*
> *God's right hand interceding for us (v. 34).*
> Who shall separate us from the love of Christ?
> *No one and nothing. No tribulation, distress, persecution, fam-*
> *ine, nakedness, danger, or sword will separate us from Christ's*
> *love (v. 35)*

Paul concludes with a firm statement of confidence: "For I
am sure . . ." (v. 38). What is Paul so certain about? That nothing
will be able to separate us from the love of God in Christ (v. 39).

To prove his point, Paul offers ten things that some might
think could separate us from Christ (vv. 38–39). "Neither death
nor life." Physical death can't separate us from God, nor can the
pain or calamities of this life. "Nor angels nor rulers." Some were

tempted to worship the angels rather than God (Col. 2:18; Rev. 22:8–9). "Rulers" refers to either heavenly beings or earthly rulers. In either case, no ruler in heaven or earth can get in the way. "Nor things present nor things to come." Nothing right now or in the future can stop God's love. "Nor height, nor depth." It doesn't matter how tall or wide the obstacle. Time (present or future) and space (height or depth) can't hurt believers. "Nor powers." No one has the strength to keep God's love from you. "Nor anything else in all creation." To cover all his bases, Paul declares that nothing in all creation can separate you from Christ's love.

Every time you act out, you might think, *How could Christ continue to love me, after I keep doing this?* But God's love is not dependent on your performance, your obedience, your thought life, your purity. It's not dependent on you *at all*.

You probably think of your performance, obedience, thought life, and purity as barriers to God's love. Christ stands on one side of the dividing wall, and you stand on the other. You don't know how to scale the wall to get to the other side. The world, your flesh, and the devil say in unison, "God's love is not for you! You're stuck over here!" But Christ knocks down these walls through his death and resurrection. For those who are predestined, called, justified, and glorified (Rom. 8:30), nothing can be an obstacle to his love.

Reflect: Your relationship with God is not dependent on the fickle nature of your love, nor anything in your life. It depends on a sure foundation: the certainty of Christ, who he is, and what he has done for you on the cross.

Reflect: How much do you rely on feelings rather than the *certainty* of God's Word that promises the *certainty* of God's love?

Act: Go to a mature Christian and make this request: "Teach me about God's love in Christ." Then soak in every truth that he or she offers.

DAY 28

Voices of Condemnation

*There is therefore now no condemnation for those
who are in Christ Jesus. (Rom. 8:1)*

AFTER PORN STRUGGLERS stumble, along with guilt and
shame, they wrestle with voices of condemnation.[1]

- "How stupid I must be to fall into the same trap."
- "How could I be a Christian if I keep doing this?"
- "How could God still love me?"
- "I'm never going to be any good to anyone."
- "You are seriously the worst. Don't even bother going back
  to God."
- "You think God will forgive you after you've given in again?
  Not a chance . . ."
- [If they are single] "No woman/man would ever want to
  marry me."
- [If they are married] "My wife/husband is going to hate me."
- "There is no chance you'll ever change."
- "What will people in church think? They'll think that I'm
  worthless."

Do you recognize any of these voices? Self-condemnation
is common after a man or woman struggles with pornography.
It's far too easy to berate yourself after you sin yet again. In fact,
it's easier to belittle yourself than to believe that God's forgiving
grace is sufficient for your foolishness.

What kind of self-talk do you speak every day? Slow down
and listen to the voices speaking loudly inside you. What you say
either helps or hurts your ability to fight this problem. Your sinful

flesh relishes any opportunity to condemn you: "Stupid! Idiot! You did it again! How could you call yourself a Christian? How could you believe that Christ loves you? There is no freedom for you! You are worthless. You might as well give up and do it again."

The flesh desires to ruin your life and trap you in your sin. But the desires of the Spirit are opposed to the flesh and at war with it (Gal. 5:17). The desires of the Spirit are for you to intimately know the love of Christ (Rom. 8:31–39), to be declared one of his children (Gal. 4:1–6), and to experience the forgiveness and freedom that come to those who trust in Christ (Luke 5:17–26; 7:36–50; Gal. 5:1).

Condemning self-talk is futile and leads you nowhere.

Repent of the bad habit of condemning yourself. If the voices keep showing up, tune them out (Prov. 1:20–21, 33). Listen to the voice of the sinless one who died for you. God says much more loudly, "Because you are united to my Son, there is no condemnation for you."

We need to reject the self-condemning words and turn up the volume on what God says. "I love you. You are mine, bought with the precious blood of my Son. When you sin, don't condemn yourself. Turn from your sin and come to me, and I'll forgive you. There is no condemnation for those who trust in my Son."

Reflect: What do you do after you stumble and look at pornography? What is your plan? What do you typically do that is unhelpful? What should you do instead?

Reflect: What kinds of damaging self-talk do you wrestle with?

Act: Write down on a sheet of paper some of the condemning things that you say to yourself. Stare at them, repent of them, pray through them, and relish the fact that there is no condemnation for God's own. Write Romans 8:1 in big letters across the bottom of the page.

DAY 29

Repentance

From that time Jesus began to preach, saying, "Repent, for the kingdom of heaven is at hand." (Matt. 4:17)

AFTER FACING SATAN in the wilderness (Matt. 4:1–11), Jesus began his preaching ministry declaring, "Repent, for the kingdom of heaven is at hand." While he could have said many things, Christ began with *repentance*.

What is repentance? It is sorrowing over what you've done wrong (2 Cor. 7:10). It's also turning away from your sin and evil, renouncing it, and turning back to God (Prov. 28:13; Ezek. 33:11). It's a change of heart and mind that leads to a new direction and new attitude (Joel 2:13; Rom. 12:2). It's a transformation of your life that results in obedience to God (1 John 2:4–6). It is grief over your ugly offense against a holy God (Ps. 51:3–4). It's a sober judgment of how small you are in light of your big God (Rom. 12:3). It's an understanding of the consequences of your sin and how it hurts your life and the lives of others (Gal. 6:7). It's a willingness to make restitution for the things you've done wrong (Luke 19:1–10). It's a willingness to turn from sin not just once but daily for the rest of your life (Matt. 3:8; Acts 26:20).

What is *not* repentance? It is not an intellectual change only. Nor is it a behavior change only. It's a heart change. It's a change of life. It starts with conviction from the Spirit and flows into a person's entire life. It is not simply feeling bad about what you did wrong and then going back to your sin. It's not a verbal acknowledgement only. You can't say sorry and then do nothing about your sin. It's not hypocrisy. You can't pretend to live a holy life on Sunday and then go home and secretly continue to commit sexual sin.

Complacency toward God will not do. The Israelites had drifted far from God, so Jesus called them to reject evil and return to God (Matt. 4:17). John the Baptist had echoed the same sentiment earlier, using the same words (Matt. 3:2). Whatever else would come later, Jesus and John called the Israelites to repentance *now*. It couldn't wait any longer.

With the arrival of Jesus, heaven had come to earth. The rule and reign of God had broken in and begun in a particular person: Christ, the Savior. Throughout the Old Testament the Israelites had heard the promise of a coming Messiah (Gen. 3:15; Ps. 2:1–12; Isa. 9:6–7; 52:13–53:13; Dan. 7:13–14; Mic. 5:2). Then there were hundreds of years of silence. But, with the arrival of Jesus, God came near again. All the promises of the prophets were fulfilled in Jesus's life, death, and ministry. God would reign sovereign on earth, and the Evil One and all the world would be brought to submission to God's Son. One day, every knee would bow and every tongue confess Jesus as Lord (Phil. 2:9–11).

Jesus emphasized repentance. You can't come back to God unless you forsake your wicked ways. You can't pretend to love God and continue to live in sin. Repent. Turn from your sin and turn to Christ in faith.

Reflect: Are you willing to forsake your sexual sin and turn back to God in faith? Let me invite you, right now, to repent of your sin.

Reflect: What obstacles or attitudes get in the way of your repentance?

Act: Go through the paragraphs about what repentance is and is not. With a highlighter, mark the things that apply to you. Find a mature believer and talk over why the unhighlighted items on the lists have not been evident in your life.

DAY 30

Faith

Now faith is the assurance of things hoped for, the
conviction of things not seen. (Heb. 11:1)

Your hope and satisfaction should come from Jesus, not from staring at people on a screen and deriving satisfaction from technology. *Walking by sight, not by faith, means you are defined by the visual world around you.* If you are enslaved to pornography, the visual world has dominated your heart and mind. And even if you are not enslaved but still struggle with pornography, you've let the visual world influence you more than it should. *Christians are called to walk by faith and not by sight.*

As encouragement to his readers, the author of Hebrews speaks of those who "endured a hard struggle with sufferings, sometimes being publicly exposed to reproach and affliction" (10:32–33). He speaks to those who went through great difficulties, pleading with them not to shrink back but to endure and persevere by faith (vv. 34–39).

He goes on to say, "Now faith is the assurance of things hoped for" (Heb. 11:1). Faith is not some blind belief or irrational commitment to something not true. Rather, faith is believing in the reality of things that we are promised. The many promises of Scripture are true, and faith knows that the things hoped for are real and solid. The promises will come to fruition. There need not be any doubt about it.

What helps believers to endure hard days and persevere? Clinging to God's promises. Not irrationally believing, but holding on to the certainty of God's promises because we know the character of him who made these promises. Thus you are called not to be sluggish or lukewarm in your Christian walk, but "through faith and patience [to] inherit the promises" (Heb. 6:12).

The author of Hebrews also says that faith is "the conviction of things not seen" (11:1). Faith is a demonstration that the unseen things are real. In our world, materialism is the defining philosophy of the day. People have confidence in what they can see or touch, not in the unseen. It's no surprise that you (and others who struggle with pornography) find hope and satisfaction through a screen, because much of the world says that this is a better way to live. But if you live by faith, you look beyond the visual and material world. You put your hope in Christ, who is seated in the heavenly realms, not in the screens that surround you. As Christians, *if we walk by faith and not by sight, we are defined by heavenly things and not by the visual world.*

As Christians, we know and trust God, who himself is invisible. The Bible teaches you not to put your hope in this visual world—especially in the naked images or videos of sex that enslave your soul. But instead put your hope in the unseen, in Christ, who has given his life for you.

Reflect: If you feel weak in your faith, remember that faith as small as a grain of mustard seed can move mountains (Matt. 17:20).

Reflect: What would it take for you to live by faith and not by sight?

Act: Write out a list of things that help you to cling to faith, and list things that tempt you to live by sight. Pray through these two lists and ask God to grow your faith.

DAY 31

The End of the Story

And I heard a loud voice from the throne saying, "Behold, the dwelling place of God is with man. . . . He will wipe away every tear from their eyes, and death shall be no more, neither shall there be mourning, nor crying, nor pain anymore, for the former things have passed away." (Rev. 21:3–4)

THERE WILL BE a day when you no longer struggle with lust or selfish desires. The battles against pornography and self-indulgent masturbation will be gone. There will be no sexual immorality, let alone sexual temptation. No more fighting images in your mind or fantasies in your heart. No more need for accountability. No more guilt or shame over looking at naked images. No more hiding or fears or false guilt or filthy feelings of being an outcast. No more hard conversations with concerned friends. No more need for internet filter programs or even electronic devices. No more anger at self or frustration with others. No more doubt about God and his character. Just no more sin or struggle anymore.

As the apostle John says, the old order of sin and death will have passed away (Rev. 21:4). The curse of Genesis 3 will be destroyed and done away with. Sin and its dreadful effects will be gone forever.

Can you imagine this? Can you even picture it in your mind? Savor this thought, because one day it will become reality. If you are struggling with pornography and masturbation (and any other form of sexual immorality), it's hard to imagine even a *porn-free* life. But take it one step further: imagine a *sin-free* life. The power that sin has over your life will be broken by the saving blood of Jesus Christ (Rev. 1:5). There will be complete freedom from guilt, shame, fears, lust, temptations, fantasies, premarital sex, and pornography.

But there is more. The absence of sin is not the best part of heaven. The most glorious part of heaven is that there will be unhindered fellowship with God for all eternity (Rev. 21:3). The only thing that will matter is that you get to be with God.

In the garden of Eden, God and man had perfect fellowship with each other, but that was lost because of the first couple's rebellion (Gen. 3). Even in a fallen world, God made his presence known in the tabernacle (Ex. 25:8), in the temple (2 Chron. 6:18), through the promises of the prophets (Isa. 7:14), and by the incarnation (John 1:14).[1] But the end of the story is that God and his children are restored to perfect fellowship with each other. They will dwell together for all eternity with no more sin, death, mourning, crying, pain, or suffering (Rev. 21:1–5).

This is the culmination of your life as well as the life of everyone who puts their trust in Christ. What a glorious day this will be!

Reflect: Do you long to be set free from the tyranny of sin? Can you picture yourself with God in eternity? Are you looking forward to being with him forever?

Reflect: Hollywood, popular books, and television make you think that heaven is about pearly gates and cute angels. But the point of heaven is God. All creation and all the supernatural creatures are oriented around the throne to worship him alone (Rev. 19:1–10).

Act: Talk, think, pray, and sing often about heaven. Having an eternal perspective that takes you beyond the circumstances of this life helps you to fight with faith. Find a good friend and share with each other about the glories of being with God in heaven.

CONCLUSION

Where Do You Go from Here?

AFTER THIRTY-ONE DAYS, we land on this important question: Where do you go from here? While volumes could be written in answer to this question, here are a few suggestions.

Stay in God's Word

Hopefully, if you've made it to the end, you have found the Word encouraging, edifying, and convicting. The call to holiness is intimidating, but you know that it's the right path.

As you fight against pornography and masturbation, your trust in God's Word is vital to your survival. Do you trust that God can bring you life? Do you believe that the One who wrote the Scriptures is for you?

Reading books and blog posts, listening to podcasts, having conversations with wise friends—all of these are good things to pursue. But the point of this devotional is to focus you on God's Word so you can come face to face with Jesus. God sent his Son for you. The reason you persevere in God's Word is so that you can be reconciled back to God through his Son.

Stay in God's Word. Dig into it and mine it for all it has to offer.

Plead with God

Pray expansive prayers. Ask for God's mercy. Ask for greater holiness. Ask for greater hope and affection for Christ.

But don't stop there. After you ask, confess. Be honest about your sin. Bring it before the Lord and bare your soul to him.

And don't stop there. Thank the Lord for what he's already

done for you, especially for what he's done for you in Christ. Express your gratitude for all the little things and big things he has done. Look for every evidence of God's grace in your life, and shout it back to him. "Thank you, God, for everything you give me!"

But don't stop there. Exalt him for who he is and what he's done. Honor him. Praise him. Adore him. Speak to God the many good things that you know about his character and what he's done for you.

Supplication. Confession. Thanksgiving. Adoration. Make them all a part of your prayers. Make this central to your battle plan for fighting against sexual sin.

Stay Close to God's People

Keep asking for help. Talk to wise friends. Be honest about sin, but also enjoy together the riches of God's grace. Let your fellowship be rich and centered on Christ.

But also make sure you stay closely connected to your church. Let its sermons sustain you (alongside your personal time in the Word). If you come in on Sunday drained from the week, let the songs, prayers, and preaching fill you up so you can go out to face a fallen world yet again. Let God's family be a safe, loving, hopeful community to help you on your journey to heaven.

Remember What God Has Done for You

Forgiveness, compassion, healing, hope, love, mercy—these are the many things that God gives you in Christ. In a fallen world, where life is often hard, busy, and frustrating, it's easy to forget the bigger things: God's glory, Jesus's death on your behalf, eternal hope, and Christ's return. And it's easy to get caught up in the small things that often demand your attention.

Don't lose sight of the cross. Fight to remember what you

have in Christ. Some days the battle against sexual sin will feel like a losing venture, but it is not. God is on your side, and the clearest evidence of this is what he has done for you in Christ. Let this gospel hope sustain you as you fight.

The End of the Matter

Jesus is always the beginning and the end of the matter. Because of what Christ has done for you—in dying on the cross for you and being raised from the grave to conquer death—you can have hope in the fight for purity. Trust in Jesus and give your life to him. He'll never disappoint you. He'll be faithful to the very end.

Acknowledgments

THANKS TO IAN Thompson, Amanda Martin, Rush Witt, and the entire team at P&R. What a privilege it is for me to publish a book with such a well-respected group. I hope this is the first of many!

I am also thankful for the elders of Capitol Hill Baptist Church, who have fought with me in the trenches as we've ushered sheep along the path to the celestial city. What a joy it is to labor with you, brothers. Thanks to Steve Boyer, Greg Spraul, and Blake Boylston, all of whom helped me with this book.

I am grateful to pastor Jason Hsieh, former intern Keith Kresge, and music man Matt Merker, all of whom have read and given me thoughtful feedback.

Thanks to the many young men and women in our congregation, who have opened up to me and let me travel with them as they fight for faith, purity, and hope.

And to Sarah, my dear wife and best friend—how much I'm indebted to you is beyond comprehension.

APPENDIX

A Brief Word on Masturbation

THE ISSUE OF masturbation deserves a brief word before we depart. Pornography and masturbation often go hand in hand. It is common for a man or woman to look at pornography, be aroused sexually, and then finish off the experience with masturbation. How should we think about masturbation as Christians?

The Problem of Masturbation

Masturbation is a problem for three reasons. First, *it's innately selfish.* Think about what you are doing: masturbation is *self*-arousal for *self*-pleasure and *self*-satisfaction. Notice how this is all oriented around *you.* Masturbation reduces sex to a kingdom of *self.* Since when has orienting anything exclusively around you been a good thing? When has selfishness led you to a closer relationship with God or greater fruit for his kingdom or better evangelism? The fundamental call of a Christian is away from oneself and to Christ. To be a Christian, you've got to think and live beyond yourself, and fundamentally for the one, true king, Jesus. Give up masturbation, because it pitifully reduces sex to a selfish act.

Second, *masturbation disregards God's purposes for sex.* Most people think of the purposes of sex as being the two Ps: pleasure and procreation (making babies). While both these reasons are certainly true, there's another reason why God gave man and woman sex to enjoy. God uses intimacy to foster unity between a man and a woman. Sex is not fundamentally about you; it is a means that God uses to build a strong bond between a man and a woman.

Think about it. When a couple is angry with each other, the last thing they want to do at that moment is have sex. They fight and work through the conflict. But what often happens after they've reconciled? Make-up sex. What's going on? After they have been divided *through conflict*, they want to be united again *through sex*. God uses intimacy—the act of physically uniting—to build emotional and spiritual unity within the marriage.

In the kingdom of God, even the pursuit of pleasure within marriage should not be self-oriented but others-oriented. When a Christian husband and wife have sex, it is not fundamentally about getting pleasure for themselves. If that were the case, they would be operating like two self-centered people within marriage. But the greater goal of sex within marriage is to serve each other. In the kingdom of God, the best sex is others-centered, not self-centered.

Third, *masturbation makes provision for the flesh, even after pornography is gone.* If a man or woman is victorious against lust and pornography, many times masturbation still lingers for months afterward. It's considered a secondary sin compared to pornography, so it is easy to rationalize continuing to masturbate. One thinks, "At least I'm not looking at pornography" or "It only affects me, so what's the big deal?" You can take nude images stored up in your mind, arouse yourself with them, and then masturbate. The desires of the flesh are to gain pleasure and satisfy yourself through sex. When you masturbate, you make provision for the flesh (Rom. 13:14). Your sinful nature is especially hungry, because you've stopped looking at pornography, and it needs someone to feed it. Masturbation accomplishes just that. It feeds your sinful nature, and whenever you feed it, it grows. Stop masturbating so that you no longer make provision for the flesh; rather, do the hard work of putting to death your sinful nature (Gal. 5:24).

What to Do about It

If you agree with my reasoning, then the next practical question is, "How do I stop it?" While there is no foolproof recipe for stopping masturbation, here are a few suggestions.

Be deliberate about your life. Passivity about sin is a deathbed. Be intentional about your thought life and your time. Strategize about how to make the best use of your days. If you are bored, don't jump online. That's bound to get you in trouble. Fill your mind and time with whatever is true, right, pure, lovely, and admirable (Phil. 4:8–9).

Recognize that the fundamentally selfish orientation of masturbation pulls you away from a life centered on Christ. You can't be selfish and Christ-centered at the same time. Fight your selfishness and pour gasoline on the flames of your desires for Christ. Get in the Word. Throw yourself into a gospel-preaching church. Fast. Pray. Pursue other believers. Grow in hope. Cherish the grace God has given you.

Accountability is crucial. You can't fight this battle on your own. Build honest, close relationships with others, and make sure that these folks ask you hard questions. Don't passively respond to your friends' inquiries. Make it your responsibility to pursue their help, which shows a level of seriousness about fighting your sin. Reach out to your accountability partners *before* you masturbate instead of *after*. Confession afterward often shows that you wanted to hold on to your sin; confession beforehand shows a greater commitment to fighting it. Be sure that you tell them what they need to know in order to make the accountability most effective. They are not mind readers. You know your heart better than they do, so let them "in" on how your heart works.

Cultivate general self-control. Masturbation is ultimately a breakdown of self-control. Discipline your mind and fight worldly pressures to conform to ungodly things (Rom. 12:2) through a deliberate pursuit of worthy subjects in reading, conversations, thoughtful media intake, and so on. Discipline your body, also, through exercise, healthy diet, and solid sleep. Is it a surprise that if you don't exercise, eat too much sugar, and lack sleep, you will be more likely to masturbate? A lazy life leaves you more vulnerable to masturbation. Self-control is a marker of a maturing faith (Gal. 5:22–23; 1 Tim. 3:2).

Squeeze everything you can out of God's Word and corporate worship. If your spiritual life is dry, dig deeply into the Word. Mine it. Dwell on it. Study it. Turn it over in your mind and heart. Let the Word of life enrich your soul. When you get to corporate worship, don't be a passive participant. Engage with the prayers; don't let your mind wander. Sing the songs with vigor, letting your love for God propel your worship. Listen to the sermon as someone who is hungry for truth. And if you are not sure how to do any of this then go to a mature Christian or your pastor and ask for help.

Confront the rationalizations that excuse your sexual sin. You feel aroused, and so you think, *I don't think I can hold it in anymore.* Right there you've created an excuse for you to masturbate. You've self-justified your sinful behavior. Don't simply tolerate these rationalizations. Confront them, label them for what they are (excuses to continue to sin), and throw them out.

Repentance needs to be quick and immediate. You've got to participate in your sanctification. God doesn't remove your sin without any fight or effort from you. The longer you wait, the more likely you are to self-justify your sexual sin. Quick and immediate repentance sharpens your conscience and helps you to fight the addictive qualities of pleasure. You can get hooked on your self-gratification. Be aggressive about repentance. With technology, there is no reason why you can't confess immediately rather than waiting until the next face-to-face meeting with an accountability partner.

Faith in Christ matters. What desires are driving your life? Your affection for the Savior, or your desire for sexual pleasure? Faith is not just knowledge of Christ; it is a wholehearted trust in Christ. Every inch of your life needs to fall under the lordship of

Christ, including your fight for sexual purity. Faith needs to sit in the driver's seat. Unbelief easily slips in and makes you vulnerable to choosing masturbation rather than purity. "God will forgive me, so I'm going to . . ." "God isn't helping anymore." "God doesn't care." These thoughts (and their many variations) are markers of unbelief. Every new day provides yet another opportunity to reject unbelief and put your faith in Christ. Cultivate your affection for your Savior. Trust in him alone.

Take practical steps to cut out the times and places you are most vulnerable. If you tend to linger in the shower or in bed in the morning, don't be surprised that you'll be more vulnerable to acting on your thoughts and sexual impulses. Get out of bed as soon as you wake up. Don't hang out in the shower. Clean yourself up quickly and then get out. If you remove these vulnerable moments, you put yourself in a better position to fight the sin overall. Think of a construction site that has signs marked on it: Danger! No entry. Let your accountability partners know where the danger zones are in your life, and start avoiding them.

If you are struggling with masturbation, know this: God is powerful, and he can change you. By God's grace, victory is possible. Don't give up or give in to masturbation. Fight it with just as much vigor as you fight your pornography struggles. Repent of this sin and give your life to Christ. He can do anything, including transform your life.

Notes

Tips for Reading This Devotional

1. Jonathan Leeman, *Reverberation: How God's Word Brings Light, Freedom, and Action to His People* (Chicago: Moody, 2011), 19.

Introduction

1. Edward T. Welch, *Addictions: A Banquet in the Grave; Finding Hope in the Power of the Gospel* (Phillipsburg NJ, P&R: 2001), 32–36.
2. Dave Furman, "Lust" (sermon, Redeemer Church of Dubai, Dubai, UAE, February 26, 2016), available online at www.redeemerdubai .com/resources/sermons/lust.
3. Furman, "Lust."
4. This does not mean, however, that Paul forgot all the good things that God had done for him. He often recounted God's faithfulness to him in the past (2 Cor. 1:10; 2 Tim. 2:13).

Day 3: Walking by the Spirit

1. Other translations of this verse include "If we live by the Spirit, we must also *follow* the Spirit" (HCSB) and "Let's keep each step in perfect sync with God's Spirit" (VOICE).

Day 5: Be Radical

1. Daniel M. Doriani, *Matthew*, Reformed Expository Commentary (Philipsburg, NJ: P&R, 2008), 1:157.

Day 7: Slay the Beast

1. This has *already* been done for you when you were born again and united to Christ. Your sins were nailed to the cross with Christ. But you are *not yet* completely rid of your sin. Christ calls on you to continue to fight the sin that dwells within you every day of your Christian life.

Day 8: God's Good News for You

1. R.C. Sproul, *Romans*, St. Andrew's Expositional Commentary (Wheaton, IL: Crossway, 2009), 158.

Day 9: Isolation

1. William Shakespeare, *King Henry VI, Part 3*, act v, scene 6.
2. Bruce K. Waltke, *The Book of Proverbs: Chapters 15–31*, The New International Commentary on the Old Testament (Grand Rapids: Eerdmans, 2005), 69.

Day 11: Good Accountability

1. As image-bearers, the most effective way to receive help is to be personally present in the other person's life.

Day 12: Bad Accountability

1. Jason Hsieh gave me this idea about ungracious accountability (email message to author, May 29, 2017).
2. Thanks again to Jason Hsieh.

Day 13: Lying to Yourself

1. Edward T. Welch, *Addictions: A Banquet in the Grave; Finding Hope in the Power of the Gospel* (Phillipsburg NJ, P&R: 2001), 182–85.

Day 16: Forgiveness in Christ

1. Remember that Satan is called "the accuser of our brothers" (Rev. 12:10).
2. Horatio G. Spafford, "It Is Well with My Soul," 1873.

Day 23: A Warning against Pride

1. Bruce K. Waltke, *The Book of Proverbs: Chapters 15–31*, The New International Commentary on the Old Testament (Grand Rapids: Eerdmans, 2005), 26–27.
2. "Humility comes before honor" (Prov. 15:33).

Day 25: Fighting Temptations

1. Leon Morris, *Hebrews*, in *The Expositor's Bible Commentary*, vol. 12,

Hebrews through Revelation, ed. Frank E. Gabelein (Grand Rapids: Zondervan, 1981), 46.

2. Do you avoid evil rather than let yourself walk down a dangerous path? Do you fight temptations with God's Word, just as Jesus did against the devil? Do you run or do you linger when temptation stares at you? Do you play with fire? Are you quick to get out as soon as possible? Are you humble enough to ask for help? Have you given up even before the temptation comes? Have you maintained vigilance even before the temptation arises?

Day 26: Shame
1. I'm indebted to Ed Welch for a lot in my life, including distinguishing between these categories of clean and unclean as they relate to shame (see "Clean and Unclean, Holy and Common," chap. 8 in his *Shame Interrupted: How God Lifts the Pain of Worthlessness and Rejection* [Greensboro, NC: New Growth Press, 2012]).

Day 28: The Voices of Condemnation
1. For more on this subject, read Heath Lambert, *Finally Free: Fighting for Purity with the Power of Grace* (Grand Rapids: Zondervan, 2013), 25–26.

Day 31: The End of the Story
1. See the note for Revelation 21:3 in the *NIV Zondervan Study Bible*, ed. D. A. Carson (Grand Rapids: Zondervan, 2015).

Suggested Resources for the Fight

Books

Chester, Tim. *Closing the Window: Steps to Living Porn Free.* Downers Grove, IL: Intervarsity, 2010. [This volume, along with the next two, is scripturally sound, practical, and written primarily for men.]

Freeman, John. *Hide or Seek: When Men Get Real with God About Sex.* Greensboro, NC: New Growth Press, 2014.

Lambert, Heath. *Finally Free: Fighting for Purity with the Power of Grace.* Grand Rapids: Zondervan, 2013.

Thorne, Helen. *Purity Is Possible: How to Live Free of the Fantasy Trap.* Epsom, UK: The Good Book Company, 2014. [Helen's book is written specifically for women struggling with sexual sin.]

Welch, Edward T. *When People Are Big and God Is Small: Overcoming Peer Pressure, Codependency, and the Fear of Man.* Philipsburg, NJ: P&R, 1997. [This book gets to the heart of sins that arise when we have an inadequate view of God.]

Workbook

Welch, Edward T. *Crossroads: A Step-by-Step Guide Away from Addiction.* Greensboro, NC: New Growth Press, 2008. [This is a short workbook that covers the basic content of Ed's full-length book on addictions. It is useful for individual study or one-on-one discipling.]

Articles and Booklets

Powlison, David. "Sexual Sin and the Wider, Deeper Battles." *The Journal of Biblical Counseling* 24, no. 2 (2006): 30–36. [David uses the image of a multiplex theatre to show that sexual sin and its causes are not simplistic, but that there are a variety of factors and heart issues behind the problem.]

Smith, Winston. *It's All about Me: The Problem of Masturbation.* Greensboro, NC: New Growth Press, 2009. [This is the best booklet on why masturbation is wrong and how to fight it.]

**BIBLICAL
COUNSELING
COALITION**

The Biblical Counseling Coalition (BCC) is passionate about enhancing and advancing biblical counseling globally. We accomplish this through broadcasting, connecting, and collaborating.

Broadcasting promotes gospel-centered biblical counseling ministries and resources to bring hope and healing to hurting people around the world. We promote biblical counseling in a number of ways: through our *15:14* podcast, website (biblicalcounselingcoalition.org), partner ministry, conference attendance, and personal relationships.

Connecting biblical counselors and biblical counseling ministries is a central component of the BCC. The BCC was founded by leaders in the biblical counseling movement who saw the need for and the power behind building a strong global network of biblical counselors. We introduce individuals and ministries to one another to establish gospel-centered relationships.

Collaboration is the natural outgrowth of our connecting efforts. We truly believe that biblical counselors and ministries can accomplish more by working together. The BCC Confessional Statement, which is a clear and comprehensive definition of biblical counseling, was created through the cooperative effort of over thirty leading biblical counselors. The BCC has also published a three-part series of multi-contributor works that bring theological wisdom and practical expertise to pastors, church leaders, counseling practitioners, and students. Each year we are able to facilitate the production of numerous resources, including books, articles, videos, audio resources, and a host of other helps for biblical counselors. Working together allows us to provide robust resources and develop best practices in biblical counseling so that we can hone the ministry of soul care in the church.

To learn more about the BCC, visit biblicalcounselingcoalition.org.